CRESSMAN
LIBRARY

CEDAR CREST
COLLEGE

Presented by

Mary Lou Green

THE JOKE SHOP

While keeping out of their father's way, Robert and Jane and Timmy unknowingly cross the invisible border into a strange and frightening world and are taken prisoner. The mysterious secret agents who call themselves Herr Brush, Mr Spock and Inspector Barlow do their best to rescue them, but without much success. The children must save themselves. But how can they? And do they altogether want to? They have fallen among ancient enemies, but they find unexpected new friends. And they learn new things: for the Dark, they discover, casts its own Light.

The
Joke Shop

By

D. J. ENRIGHT

CHATTO & WINDUS · LONDON

Published by
Chatto & Windus Ltd
40–42 William IV Street
London WC2N 4DF

★

Clarke, Irwin & Co. Ltd
Toronto

© D. J. Enright 1976

ISBN 0 7011 5097 1

Printed and bound in Great Britain by
REDWOOD BURN LIMITED
Trowbridge & Esher

CONTENTS

'Our acts our angels are, or good or ill,
Our fatal shadows that walk by us still.'

1 · *The Trouble with Father*

'I'm stuck! It's not going to come out,' they heard their father raging desperately as they vanished into the front garden. 'Who's going to pay for your next lot of plimsolls? That's what I'd like to know.'

'What are plimsolls?' Timmy asked.

'Ocean liners,' said Robert, who was older and clever and knew a lot of things, but wasn't always right. Sometimes he found it less boring to be wrong.

'Perhaps we're going on a sea voyage,' suggested Jane, who came in between the boys, and was inclined to be hopeful.

'On a crew?' asked Timmy.

'The word is *cruise*,' Robert said. 'Actually.'

Timmy nodded. It made sense. A big ship would need to have a lot of sailors, one crew wouldn't be enough.

But really they knew the truth of the matter. Their father was writing another book, and therefore they had to watch their peas and queues. That was what it came down to.

When he was writing a book, Daddy was rather sweet — such was Jane's view — and didn't make a fuss when they stayed out late. He didn't even notice. Robert, though, was of the opinion that at such times their father was distinctly bad-tempered: at least when he

9

noticed them, which was what counted. Noticing them seemed to interfere with his work. Which he, Robert, thought was a bit odd, since the books he wrote were meant to be for children.

'Perhaps, when you think about it, it's not *really* odd,' Timmy remarked. He didn't quite know what he meant by this, but he had observed that it usually had the effect of stopping tiresome arguments about the odd behaviour of grown-ups.

Trees and grass, Robert reflected, that was all there was, in the school holidays. Just trees and grass. Children were supposed to be mad keen on them, for some reason. As in his father's stories, for example. Still, now that the rain had stopped, it was a fine day, as people said, a reasonably fine day, and the sun was shining, mainly on trees and grass.

They decided to walk across the common to the outskirts of the town. There were some shops there worth looking into. Small ones, old and special, and not too well lighted — very different from the great, glaring, all-the-same supermarkets in the town centre. And they might see that funny-looking person again, with his large pipe decorated with tassels, and his short cape and leather knickerbockers.

Timmy was pleased to have got that last word right, since he didn't always, and told his brother and sister that in his opinion the funny person was a Bewarean pheasant, judging by appearances.

'Pleasant, I should think,' Jane remarked.

'Peasant, actually,' said Robert.

'Oh well, not really odd,' said Timmy, 'when you come to think about it.'

2 · *A Brush with the Law*

There the interesting person was, sitting on a bench in front of what had once been the village hall, before the town reached out for the village. The hall now had a big sign outside: 'BINGO EVERY NIGHT'.

'A foxy pheasant,' said Timmy.

'Peasant,' Robert reminded him.

'Poxy peasant,' muttered Timmy, suspecting that he was saying something very rude.

'But he *does* look pleasant,' Jane said hopefully. She rather liked older people, and felt safer when they were around. More than the others, she missed their mother, who had gone to Kensington, in London, to look after Granny who was mildly unwell. Granny refused to come to them, because she had always lived in London and was afraid of the country. If you positively wanted animals, she said, there was a zoo in London – and that was enough, that was quite bad enough. For her part Granny preferred to go to the theatre and suffer in comfort.

'Won't you sit down, my dears,' said the foxy fellow, pointing to the bench rather grandly. 'I won't bite you.'

They didn't believe he would, so they sat down.

'Hair brush,' he then remarked. The children nodded politely, and Timmy wondered whether this was meant

11

as a rebuke for him, and patted his hair down.

'Oh no.' The old gentleman stroked his nose. 'H-e-r-r. . .
Herr Brush is my name, as it happens.'

They told him their names. 'Not as nice as yours,'
Robert said, extra-politely.

'Personally, I'd really rather be a Pun than a Hun,'
their new friend remarked. He went on to tell them about
two great friends of his, the Pun Pair, who lived in the
Pundreds.

'Lot of punting goes on there, you know. In fact he is
the Master of the Punt, and she is the Mistress of the
Pounds. Punting and pounding every weekend, during
the season. A beautiful sight. Not to mention sound.'

'Don't you mean hunting?' Robert queried.

'Good gracious no!' exclaimed Herr Brush, whose nose
had turned quite pale. 'I wouldn't tip my tail to a *hunter*!
Punning with the hare is more in my line. . . I say, that
was good, wasn't it — didn't you hear a pun fall?'

'No, I didn't. Did you?' Robert turned to Jane.

'I don't *think* I did,' she said, not wishing to contradict
the gentleman. 'Did you drop one?'

'I can hear a foot fall.' Timmy was rather pleased
with himself.

They looked up and there stood a tall slim man, with
a very thoughtful expression.

'Good morrow, my friend,' said Herr Brush in his
grand manner. He introduced the children to his 'excellent friend, Mr Spock'.

'Sometimes I call him Mr Spick and Span, because he
is.'

'How do you do, Mr Spick,' said Timmy, on his best
behaviour. 'Pleased to meet you, Mr Span.'

'Mr Spock,' said Robert and Jane severely.

12

'I thought for a moment you might be the Lacey children,' said Mr Spock, sounding faintly disappointed. He then said something to Herr Brush in an undertone.

'Really? Oh dear me,' Herr Brush replied. 'That's dreadfully worrying for the poor woman. Do you think it could be. . .? It doesn't *have* to be. . .'

He looked at the children. 'Do you happen to have seen any Lacey children recently, my dears?'

Timmy certainly hadn't seen any lacy children. He had only noticed one boy since they had left the house, and he was more raggedy than lacy.

'I don't think we know them,' said Jane. 'We haven't been here long. We used to live in London, but our father couldn't work there, so we had to move.'

'He's a writer,' Robert explained, a mite apologetically. 'He writes books.'

'Children's books,' said Timmy, as if honesty forced him to add insult to injury. 'But it's very difficult to write books for children. You can't do it just any old where.'

'Ah,' said Mr Spick, or Span, or Spock. 'Children. Yes, it must be truly difficult. My brother knows more about children than I do. He's a Doctor.'

'Do only sick children read books?' asked Timmy, knowing it was polite to show interest.

'Don't be silly, Timmy,' Robert said. 'You don't have to be sick to read a book.'

'I was given a big book, a big Annal, when I had measles,' Timmy protested. 'With pictures in it, and puzzles. I was very sick then.'

'I'm sure it helps,' said Mr Spock, smiling amiably.

Herr Brush was plainly worrying about something. 'Who is − er − on the job? Inspector Barlow?'

13

The other man nodded. 'A pity that Inspector Barlow doesn't more obviously *like* children, I always think,' said Herr Brush.

'I don't think it matters in the least,' Mr Spock said. 'Inspector Barlow likes things to be in their proper places, and that's what counts. As long as his mind is in the right place, it doesn't matter where his heart is.'

But Herr Brush didn't look at all happy. 'Poor little things. Poor little lost Laceys. . .'

'*You* are all heart,' Mr Spock told him in a severe tone of voice.

'And thereby hangs a tale,' Herr Brush murmured mournfully. Or perhaps it was tail. 'Dear children,' he said, 'I think you had better run straight off home. In fact I think I had better come with you and make sure you get there safely.'

The children glanced at one another. They had no intention of going home yet awhile.

'Ho,' said Herr Brush, brightening up. 'I see we're in for a Brush with the Law. Here's the Inspector in person.'

*   *   *

Robert and Jane thought of making a dash for it, but it was too late. The Inspector was a large man with a large and red face which could have been friendly except for the fierce expressions which its owner imposed on it. The children felt that they were surrounded, as far as they could be surrounded by one person.

'I'm looking for two children, not three,' said the Inspector in an aggrieved tone. 'Must be two because they are alleged to be twins. The two twin children of the widow-woman Lacey who lives in Shoe Lane.' After a pause for the children's iniquity to sink in, he continued.

14

'Approximately the age of this person.' He pointed to
Jane. 'In fact Lily is twelve – and the other twin, known
as Leslie, is – oh, what is he now?'

'Twelve?' suggested Timmy.

'Something like that,' the Inspector conceded. 'At all
events, their mother doesn't know what to do. She's
distraught. Not to say prostrate. Highly upset she is.
Just because she's lost her children and doesn't know
where to find them.'

Another pause. 'What a fuss about two *children!* I'd
be glad myself – cock-a-hoop, you might say – if someone stole my child. Even more so if they stole my children. Happy as a sandboy I'd be –'

'You know you don't mean that, Inspector,' wailed
Herr Brush. The children noticed a large tear about to
roll down his long nose. 'You don't really mean it.'

'Since, Inspector, you have no children,' Mr Spock remarked coldly, 'no one is likely to steal them and therefore you are not going to feel either happy or unhappy
about it. There is a curious lack of logic about your
argument. I find it quite fascinating.'

Timmy liked the sound of that. Quite masterly, he
thought.

'Either way we shouldn't be standing here talking,'
cried Herr Brush, who was sitting. He sprang to his feet,
wrapping his cloak around him. 'We must search for the
missing kiddies. Who knows what. . .' He glanced at the
children and stopped. 'Little pictures have big fears.'

'I've looked everywhere, and I haven't found a trace
of them,' snorted the Inspector, a look of wounded in-
dignation on his capacious face. 'Neither hair nor hide.'

Timmy had decided he wanted to be like Mr Spock
when he grew up. An earlier ambition, which he now

15

despaired of realizing, was to be one of those lovable children who advertised baked beans, hamburgers or footwear on television. But now he would simply be cool, clever and slightly incredulous.

'You can't have looked *everywhere,* else you would have found them,' he said coolly. 'They must be *somewhere.*'

'Unless they are nowhere,' said Mr Spock softly, disappointing Timmy rather.

'Exactly!' shouted the Inspector.

'Oh dear, oh dear,' lamented Herr Brush, wiping the tip of his nose.

'Why do you go round looking for children if you don't like them?' Timmy tried to retrieve lost ground.

'Oh Timmy, you are so rude!' said his sister.

'It's because his mother is away,' Robert explained. 'He always gets a bit above himself then.'

'Why?' roared the Inspector, frightening Timmy out of his coolness. 'Why? You ask *why*? You're no better than a child!' He paused to let this reprimand sink in. 'I'll tell you for why. Because it is my job. J-O-B. Because it's my duty. See? My du. . . tea. . . A cup of tea. . . I haven't touched a cup of tea since yesterday. Called out at creak of dawn. No breakfast, no nothing.' He sighed noisily. 'I can't go looking for lost children on an empty stomach. It's more than flesh and blood can stand.'

The Inspector turned and hurried away after casting a very black look at the children, Timmy in particular.

'Come on,' said Herr Brush. 'Including you, dear children. But you must stay close to us, no running off on your own. It's not true that darkning doesn't strike twice in the same spot, you know.'

'A good idea,' Mr Spock said, 'psychologically valid. Set a child to catch a child.'

3 · Joke of the Month

'Let's look everywhere,' said Timmy enthusiastically.

'And nowhere, too,' said Mr Spock. 'Don't forget nowhere.'

'They won't be in the supermarket,' Robert reckoned.

'And they can't have fallen into the river,' said Jane cheerfully, 'because there isn't one for miles.'

'I know another place where they won't be,' Timmy announced. 'They won't be at school.'

'Quite,' said Mr Spock. 'If they were at school they wouldn't be missing.'

'I only meant it's the holidays and the schools are closed.'

'You see, my dear Brush, how right we were? These young people may prove of invaluable assistance to us.'

'Indeed,' murmured Herr Brush, looking brighter. 'The pitter-patter of tiny footpads. . .'

*　　*　　*

The first shop they came to was a baker's. There was nothing much to be seen there — only three small dusty-looking cakes and a queue of three large housewives.

A little further along the street was the old joke shop, with grimy windows, which never seemed to be open for custom.

'What if somebody wants to buy something?' Timmy had once asked.

'Then they can't — that's the joke,' Robert had explained.

The children had never altogether liked the joke shop, though they always found themselves stopping to look in the window when they passed that way. There were strange things to be seen through the dirt.

There was a pretended ink blot to leave on your mother's best tablecloth. Hideous false noses, bigger even than Herr Brush's. A large black spider with furry legs and nasty red eyes. Plastic maggots which writhed about if you squeezed a rubber ball. A pistol which fired a cigarette which blew up when you — or preferably someone else — smoked it. Vampire's teeth, called 'Dracula's Dentures', sold in pairs, with bloodstains attached. A back-scratcher with human-looking fingernails at the scratching end. A tumbler guaranteed to spill its contents down your chin when you tried to drink from it, and another, containing coloured liquid, which you were guaranteed to be unable to drink from at all.

There were some things the children didn't fancy in the least, and wrinkled their noses at. Little cushions, for instance, which made rude noises when sat on. And though they hadn't once caught sight of the owner, or of anyone else, from time to time the wares on show were changed. At least something called 'THE JOKE OF THE MONTH' was. Once it had been an article looking very much like what badly trained dogs leave behind them on the pavement.

This time it was something they couldn't make out — a mysterious object made of black material, resembling a tube with a magnifying glass at the end, except that

19

the glass was black and concave. The sign said: 'Machine For Casting Shadows Without Light. Amaze Your Friends! Take Umbrage Now! Stocks Strictly Limited! It Is Darker Than You Think!!'

Timmy was sure that Mr Spock would be able to explain the mysterious machine to them, but the two grown-ups were talking together in an undertone, paying no attention to the shop window.

Jane shivered — it didn't seem a very funny joke, whatever it was — and they moved on.

Next came a wine shop. The manager was holding a large flagon up to the light and talking to a customer.

'A pleasing little wine. You can see right through it. That's the acid test. . . .'

They both stared at it thoughtfully.

'It travels well, too,' said the wine merchant.

'Oh, I only live a few doors away,' said the customer.

*   *   *

They had passed an empty space where there had once been a shop selling musical instruments. It had been bombed flat in the war, their mother had told them, and there was a story that sometimes late at night sad music could be heard there.

They arrived at an ice-cream parlour well-known to Timmy.

'They might be in there,' he ventured.

'Hardly,' remarked Mr Spock. 'The window extends the whole length of the interior, there are no corners hidden from view, and there is no back room. Also there is quite obviously nobody there at all.'

'Little pitchers have big mouths,' Herr Brush said, 'and I think I know what the dear child intends. The

20

creaminal mentality, if you get my drift.' He winked vigorously.

'It will be quite all right for me to have a Giant Everest Eat-it-because-it-is-There Sundae Special,' Timmy told the company reassuringly. 'It comes with a Best Biscuit. . . Mind you, I like all sorts,' he added, 'all and sundae.' Then he remembered his manners. 'Jane prefers a Strawberry Cornet with Chocolate Sauce and Robert likes a Coffee Cornet with a Dash of Vanilla on top.'

So they went in, and Timmy ordered the ice-creams. Herr Brush asked if he might have a warmish Pepsi-Cola, seeing that ices made his front teeth ache, but Mr Spock chose a plain vanilla with wafers.

'Most interesting,' he commented, without much enthusiasm, adding that it was the first ice-cream he had ever consumed. The children smiled — he must have been joking. But Herr Brush told them no, it was quite true: where Mr Spock came from they had neither ice nor cream.

'Nor Sundays,' said Mr Spock.

Timmy wondered whether he really wanted to grow up to be like Mr Spock after all. Not at any rate, he decided, till he was much older than at present.

'It's your ears,' Timmy remarked. 'I knew there was something funny about your face. . .'

'Shush, Timmy,' said Jane. 'You know it's rude to. . .'

'I don't mind,' Mr Spock said rather sadly. He was aware that his ears were larger and more pointed than was commonly the case in that part of the universe.

'I think they're rather beautiful,' put in Jane. 'Like sea-shells. . .'

'Or ice-cream cornets,' said Timmy, feeling he had

21

gone and spoilt his chances of a second treat. 'Quite fas'nating, really.'

Herr Brush considered that some explanation might be in order.

'You see, our friend Mr Spock is somewhat unusual. Like your favourite ice-cream, he is a mixture, a − if I may say so − a hybrid.'

'Very highbred I should think.' Timmy was all out to appease and placate.

'Thank you, Timmy,' said Mr Spock, who in fact did have an aristocratic look about him.

'Mr Spock is not wholly of this place. His parents, bless them, were different − different from each other, that's to say. Of different − er − races. Or, you might even say, different worlds. A most happy conjunction, if I may take the liberty, though in fact my ears are just as long as his. Less shell-like, it may be, but. . .'

In fact Mr Spock's father came from the planet Vulcan, where Mr Spock had spent the formative years of his youth, but Herr Brush didn't wish to be too personal. Vulcan had a bad name hereabouts. Either people thought it was made of vulcanite throughout, or else, if they were better read, that it was entirely populated by hard-faced steel-workers. There were even some − though the children may not have been among them − who believed that the very existence of the planet Vulcan had been astronomically discredited. And the evidence of Mr Spock and his external appearance would hardly be sufficient to change their minds. 'They can't believe their own eyes,' Herr Brush had once observed to him, 'let alone your ears.' Mr Spock had merely looked pained.

'Yes,' Mr Spock now interrupted, clearly embarrassed by all this talk about himself. 'Yes, you could say

22

there's a touch of the star-brush about me.'

'I *see*,' said Jane.

'We see,' said Timmy, who certainly didn't, but it sounded a rather fine thing to have about you. 'Hair-brush and star-brush — we *are* lucky to have met you both. . .' His gaze fell dolefully towards his empty plate.

'Why not? It might be a good idea for them to get something solid inside them, don't you think, Mr Spock?' said Herr Brush. 'Just in case.'

'Something solid? Is that what you call it? Oh well, it can't do any harm, I imagine.'

So they had a second helping all round, except for Mr Spock who muttered something indistinct and incomprehensible about having once been stranded on a badly frozen planet and finding nothing but ice-plants to eat for months on end.

Jane remarked that Inspector Barlow did seem very fond of tea.

'Brand-tea and whisk-tea I wouldn't be at all surprised,' said Timmy censoriously, thinking of the Inspector's red face and uncertain temper.

'Thou knowest this man's fall,' Herr Brush uttered the words solemnly, 'but thou knowest not his wrestling. . .'

'I bet he's a jolly good wrestler,' said Timmy more charitably. 'One of the good *bad* ones who you want to lose, like Mick McManus or Bobby Barnes. But sometimes they win, and then you can boo them.'

Herr Brush explained to them that poor Inspector Barlow had to drink a lot of tea because he couldn't afford anything stronger. The fact was, not so long ago the Inspector had submitted an official claim for a wage increase of 137% to enable him to fight the economic crisis more successfully. When the Chief Constable, who

23

was even larger and redder than the Inspector, declined rather firmly to oblige him, he promptly went on strike.

Then what happened, did they think? While the Inspector was marching smartly backwards and forwards in front of the Police Station, carrying a banner which read 'CRIME PAYS – THE LAW DON'T' on one side and 'SPARE A COPPER' on the other, his house was burgled brutally by a person or persons unknown – and subsequently unapprehended. They took his television set, his treasured first-edition copy of *The Adventures of Sherlock Holmes* autographed by Dr Watson himself, his collection of foreign stamps featuring famous police inspectors, his drinks cabinet (with the drinks inside it), and his wife's vintage sewing-machine.

'A savage blow it was,' commented Herr Brush. 'A blow from which a lesser man might never have recovered.'

So then the Inspector called off the strike, voluntarily accepted a 19% reduction in salary because of the economic crisis, and returned to work.

'I'm afraid it hasn't improved his temper,' Herr Brush concluded sadly.

The children laughed politely, with a tentative, regretful sort of laugh, but Robert and Jane didn't for a moment believe Herr Brush's story was true. Timmy mostly believed things, at any rate if they were told by people he liked, despite his efforts not to, and he felt quite sorry for the Inspector, especially for losing his television set.

Robert asked why it was the Inspector didn't like children.

'It's not as simple as that,' answered Herr Brush. 'You might say, as the Bard once did, that his nature is subdued to what it works in, like the dyer's hand.'

'Oh,' Jane said politely, wondering if perhaps the children the Inspector had experienced were particularly grubby ones.

'I fear my friend Brush is speaking obscurely,' Mr Spock said. 'Let us put it this way. . . . Young people like you have spots on their faces. Not invariably, of course — and present faces excepted, I have no doubt. I am speaking, as you will understand, metaphorically. Older people, however, sometimes have spots on their *brains*. They may also have spots on their faces too, but that is beside the point. They have — *mutatis mutandis* — spots on their brains. Tender places where they have been prodded too often and too hard —'

'Achilles' heels, if you prefer,' broke in Herr Brush. 'Where the shoe pinches. A thorn in the side. A red rag to a bull. Or a shorn lamb.'

'That, I would say,' said Mr Spock, 'is the fact of the matter where the estimable Inspector is concerned.'

'Oh,' said Robert and Jane.

Timmy had no intention of prodding Inspector Barlow's brain, or any other part of him.

'Does he think it was children who did it?' That would account for his low opinion of them, Timmy supposed.

'Did what?' asked Herr Brush, who had forgotten the tale he had just been spinning.

'The stealing?'

'Children stealing? Dear heavens, no! Rather the other way around, I much fear.'

'So do I,' said a large red face, so startling Timmy that the last mouthful of ice-cream went down the wrong way.

'I fear you gentlemen have been neglecting your duty in the execution of pleasure,' Inspector Barlow continued, brushing a few drops of tea off his uniform. 'I should have expected Herr Brush to be combing the streets and Mr Spock to be spurring after the spoliators.'

Looking guilty, Herr Brush and Mr Spock got up — 'And I should have expected these — children — to be safely at home in their bosom by now,' added the Inspector — and they all filed out of the ice-cream parlour.

4 · *The Shadow Cabinet*

Now, as they approached the common, the three men were deep in discussion. What they could hear of it the children couldn't understand.

'No doubt that clever Mr Le Carré, him with the spy stories, could soon put us right. Microphones hidden in standard lamps, ho ho.' That was the Inspector. 'Or that Mr Deighton. Not to mention Mr Fleming. . . oh yes. . .'

'Who, what. . .?' Mr Spock was being puzzled.

'No comparison whatsoever,' Herr Brush expostulated. 'Any fool can cross one of *those* piddling frontiers. . . Diplomatic representation even. . . Can you imagine, their man at the Court of St James. . .'

'Who, what. . .?'

'Entirely different,' Herr Brush sounded indignant. 'No cloak, no dagger. Hand to mouth. Or do I mean hand over fist? Bound hand and foot? Off the cuff, most certainly. . .'

Mr Spock was saying something in his most reasonable voice about the nature of things and the futility of kicking against the pricks. Empiric, he remarked, pragmatic.

'No glory. . .' That was the Inspector. 'No promotion. . .'

The children looked at one another and, without a

word, silently but swiftly took another direction. They didn't consider it a good idea at all to be taken home. Their father wouldn't be pleased to see them escorted by a big short-tempered police officer and two other persons who, it had to be admitted, might seem a little strange to anyone who didn't know them.

'I think there's something funny about that joke shop,' said Robert when they had covered a safe distance.

Timmy restrained himself from remarking that you would expect there to be something funny about a joke shop.

'Me too,' said Jane. 'You know, for a moment, when we were standing outside, I had a queer feeling there were more of us than there were.'

'I'd like to know how that machine for making shadows works,' Timmy said. It might be useful at school when they were asking questions you didn't know the answers to.

'But let's hurry and get there before the sun goes in,' Robert said, not very sure of the wisdom of it all.

*   *   *

It seemed to them that the sign wasn't the same as when they were there before. 'Shadow Cabinet — This Way To The Umbraculum — Special Ice-Cream Free Within!' Otherwise everything was as it had been, the spider rendered harmless by a thick coating of dust, the mechanical mouse looking more black than white.

'What's a um-brac-u-lum?' asked Timmy.

'Look!' Jane was pointing at something at the back of the window. 'What's that? Do you see?'

'That's just our reflections,' Robert answered after a moment.

28

'There are three of us — and only two reflections.'

Timmy jumped up and down in case he was too small to have a reflection. There were still only two reflections, though.

'You're right,' said Robert, having looked behind them in case someone was standing there. 'They seem to be waving to us.'

Timmy waved back. 'Do you think they could be the lacy children everybody's looking for?' Maybe there was a reward for finding them.

But they couldn't be children at all. They were only reflections in the grimy glass, dim reflections of children who couldn't possibly be there.

'Perhaps they're joke children.' Timmy wasn't feeling at all brave. 'Just joke children. Like the spider isn't really a spider, and the ink blot on the table-cloth isn't really an ink blot, only pretended. P'raps it's just another thingi-jig — another no-velty. . .'

At that moment there came a faint clicking sound from the shop door, which they saw was now standing ajar. There was no one to be seen.

'If the door's open, we'd better go in and look, I suppose,' Robert said, reluctantly.

'It's black in there,' Timmy said reproachfully. He thought they ought to go home after all. It was beginning to grow dark outside, so what would it be like inside?

But the others were moving towards the door, and he wasn't going to be left alone.

29

5·'Where are we?'

They had no sooner entered than the door swung to and closed with a firm click. It was indeed very dark inside.

Then they saw the two faintly glimmering faces they had glimpsed in the window.

'We were waving to warn you to go away,' said the two glimmers in faint voices. 'They made us stand here, to trap you. They held us. We did try to warn you.'

'Who are you?' asked Robert.

'Who are *they*?' asked Timmy, which was less polite but, he felt, more to the point.

'Where are we?' asked Jane.

'We're the Lacey twins,' the Lacey twins told them, 'Lily and Leslie —'

The children became aware of indistinct shadowy figures closing in on them.

'Come with us,' one of them said softly.

Though the children tried hard to pull away, they couldn't escape. Robert fought, but his fists seemed to go right through the shapes, and he could feel his strength fading away.

Somehow or other, though no force was used, the children found themselves moving down a long black corridor. It was strange and frightening, like the first time they had been on an escalator in the London

Underground, fearful of falling either forwards or backwards, and being carried on helplessly all the time.

* * *

It was as if they were travelling through a wood at midnight. Yet when they bumped into the trees, they felt nothing, or only the faintest sensation, like gliding effortlessly through a cloud of cobwebs.

'The Shadeau,' murmured one of their captors. And as they came nearer they could distinguish the dim outlines of a castle, large and gloomy and (they felt) rather horrid. Pale battlements and turrets which let the darkness through, a starless and moonless sky, and then a gate which slowly opened. It closed behind them with thin, disturbing creaks and groans.

They were taken into a large room — they could hardly make out the walls or the ceiling — which they later found was the Dunkelkammer, where important meetings were held. It was impossible to tell how many people were present — people or whatever they were, for they resembled people in their general shape, but moved differently, more smoothly, and seemed to have no expressions on their faces. It passed through Robert's mind that they might be wearing stocking-masks.

A figure, as wraith-like as the others but unusually tall, came forward to look at them.

'Welcome. Welcome to the Land of the Shadows.' The voice was thin and not especially welcoming.

'I don't like it much here,' whispered Timmy, reaching for his sister's hand. The three of them joined hands, yet they could scarcely feel the hands they were holding.

'That,' said the figure with a trace of spectral amusement, 'is immaterial. Like so much else here.'

31

His face was still, his eyes were like dead diamonds.

He motioned them to sit down on a couch, and it seemed that as they sank into it, it sank into them. In silence someone brought them shadowy cakes to eat, which Robert and Jane left untouched. Easy on the teeth, thought Timmy, who had a loose one, but not what he would call tasty. There was ice-cream too, and fright always made him feel hungry, but it melted before he could get his tongue round it.

The tall figure had apparently finished his examination of them. 'That will do for the present,' they heard him say, in a voice like a breeze rustling through leaves, as he left the chamber. 'Highly satisfactory. A good night's work.'

*   *   *

The children were told that they would now be taken to their quarters. They had no idea how far they travelled from the chamber, for they could not tell how fast they were moving, and there seemed no way of judging distances in this land.

The Lacey twins were waiting for them. Once the door was locked behind them, Robert asked the twins how long they had been there.

'It must be,' said Lily, 'five or ten years at least,' said Leslie.

They went on to tell, between them, of how one day long ago they had tried the door of the joke shop and it had opened at once. They had been looking at the funny things in the window. The spider, the mouse, the imitation ink blot, the flower-in-the-buttonhole which squirted water when you squeezed a hidden bulb. And there was a notice there which caught their attention:

32

'Reduced Terms For Twins And Other Small Parties —
Enquire Within!!!'

'We *are* twins,' said Lily defensively, 'and our circumstances *are* reduced,' said Leslie. 'And it was raining,'
Lily said, 'and we'd got nothing to do,' Leslie said.

Once they were inside the shop the door closed to,
locking itself. Then they realized they were not alone.

'Our mum must be,' said Lily, 'ever so upset,' said
Leslie. 'We are all she's got,' they said together. Tiny
shimmering tears trickled down their pale cheeks.

Jane told them that everybody was looking for them,
including a large and important policeman, so it couldn't
be long now before they were all rescued and safely
back at home.

'You two look very shadowy to me,' Timmy put in
suspiciously.

That made the Lacey twins cry a little more. They
didn't have the strength to cry very vigorously, it seemed.

'Oh Timmy, do shut up!' cried Robert, looking hard
at him. 'Anyway, a pot shouldn't call a kettle black.'
Timmy was sure he had said no such thing.

'When you came into the shop,' said Lily, 'you were
so solid and strong-looking,' added Leslie reproachfully.
'But you're fading already,' said Lily sadly, 'so there,'
concluded Leslie.

'My mother says I'm very well-built for my age,'
Timmy retorted, putting out his tongue.

'We mustn't quarrel,' said Robert firmly. 'We must
stick together.'

They all agreed, and the twins described their
experiences.

Ever since entering the shop they had felt themselves
growing fainter and fainter, at least their bodies. Growing

more and more like the inhabitants of that country. For it was a country, or perhaps it was a whole world, and though they had seen little of it, they had learnt much about it.

'Like being in school?' Jane asked.

Yes, it was like being in school. In fact most of the time they *were* in school, having lessons, hours and hours of them. But in these lessons everything was different, different from what they had learnt before. Or perhaps sometimes it wasn't: the twins had mostly forgotten their old lessons.

'But we haven't forgotten,' Lily said, 'about our mum,' Leslie said. 'And we still want to go back to our home,' said Lily, 'even if we can't remember much about it,' Leslie added.

The Shadows weren't exactly cruel to them, the twins said, but they were cold and stern, and the twins lived in a state of vague fearfulness.

But what did the Shadows, since that was what they called themselves, want of the children? As far as the twins could tell, all they wanted of the children was the children themselves.

Robert wondered whether it couldn't be a kidnapping gang, really, there was a lot of that about, and their parents would be told how much money to pay for their return.

'Our mum wouldn't pay any money,' said Lily dejectedly, 'to get us back,' said Leslie. Together they added: 'Because she hasn't got any.'

Robert had a horrid vision of his father putting the unopened ransom note among the other bills, the electricity and the telephone and the water and the rates, and forgetting all about it.

'I expect they just want to have us around,' Timmy said in a brave voice, as if that were the most natural desire in the world, in any world.

'But all the time we're getting more and more like them,' moaned Lily. 'And soon we won't be able to go home even if we could,' Leslie added tearfully. 'Look at us,' cried Lily. 'And look at you, too,' Leslie cried, 'it's happening to you as well.'

They fell silent, except for Timmy sniffing back his tears.

'Still,' said Leslie, who had been groping about for the bright side, 'if you fall down, you don't hurt your knees.'

Timmy thought that sounded rather pleasant, at least, since he didn't like iodine (his father swore by it, saying you could actually feel the death pangs of the microbes) or elastoplast either (his father had a theory about that too: that it didn't hurt if you yanked it off at one go. But it did).

'I don't s'pose you could be spanked,' he remarked. 'Not so it hurt.'

'No,' said Leslie, 'because you can fall all the way down the stairs and when you get there, the bottom is just as soft as the step you fell off.'

But no one was cheered for long by the thought. Timmy asked himself how you would know you had stopped falling if you didn't hit something and feel a hurt somewhere. How would you know you weren't dead even? He pinched his arm: he could feel it, but it didn't hurt as much as it ought. He tapped his head cautiously against the wall, and it was like sinking into a bag of beans.

'Let me show you,' offered Leslie, and gave him a jab in the stomach with his elbow. It was painful enough to make Timmy swing at the boy's head with all his strength. Nothing happened. Leslie smiled weakly, and Timmy's fist tickled slightly: that was all.

'See?' said Leslie with sad pride.

Robert had been examining the bars across the window. They didn't look all that strong. But when he tried to grip them in his hands and bend them, he couldn't make them budge.

'We tried that,' Lily said. 'We've tried everything,' Leslie said. 'And when you've been here as long as we have, the bars and the doorknobs will show through your hands.'

It appeared to have grown darker, if that was possible. The children held one another's hands; at least they tried to. Timmy cried a little, very quietly. Before long they fell asleep.

6 · *Eldest of Things*

When they awoke, the darkness was less intense. It was hardly light, but more a shadow of a shade of light. Like the first sign of dawn.

They found that food had been left for them: cool glasses of what looked like blackcurrant juice but tasted more like orange, and bowls of cereal. The cereal may have been Rice Krispies, though it didn't go snap, crackle, pop, but the milk was black in colour. So were the bread and the butter and the marmalade. Whatever the colour, and despite the lack of flavour, they felt better after they had eaten.

But then the person, the shape, who had inspected them on the previous evening entered the room. The Lacey twins were sent away to their lessons.

'You will meet again soon,' said the Shadow softly. Then he turned to Robert, Jane and Timmy. 'Will you be able to understand explanations?' he asked. 'Are explanations necessary? Do I need to throw – as you would say, throw light – on the situation?'

'Yes,' said Robert stoutly. 'We would like more light.'

'That is something you will soon learn to do without – easily and gladly.'

'But we can't *see* properly! And it makes us feel sick.'

'You will soon be able to see everything which is

37

worthy of being seen.' They noticed that he was wearing dark glasses, as if distressed by what little glimmering of light there was. 'And you will soon feel well again.'

'Why can't we go home?' asked Jane, her voice trembling.

'This will be your home. And a better one.'

'But why?' asked Robert. 'What do you want us for?'

'Shadows we are, and Shadows we pursue. Why else should we want you, young children as you are — neither important statesmen nor famous scientists? You have no military secrets to give us, and you cannot transform our economy for us. Nor, as far as I know' — what may have been a thin grin came over his lips — 'are you great football players or three-minute milers. . .'

'Robert's a jolly good dribbler,' put in Timmy loyally, 'and my father is teaching Jane to play chess —'

'Ah yes, your father. . . A writer of stories for children, mere shadows of shadows. . .'

'He very nearly won a prize once,' Timmy boasted.

'The only real prizes are here.'

'But *why*?' Robert insisted. 'You still haven't said why you brought us to this place.'

The dim luminosity had faded now, and the Shadow removed his dark glasses.

'It is a law of nature that like seeks to increase like — that Shadows seek to increase Shadows, to multiply. It is a law of our land that the land should strive to grow greater. This is not a question of deliberating or planning, but pure instinct. We want you because it is in our nature to want you.'

He paused briefly, then continued in a softer tone, as if speaking amusedly to himself. 'Though we do not lack our share of thinkers to supply us with fine reasons for doing what nature obliges us to do — with policies to explain and justify what is beyond the need for explanation or justification.'

He paused again. 'You children are not stupid, far from it. Which is why we would rather have you as friends than as enemies. And alas there appears to be no third alternative, as yet. . . But it cannot be expected that you should understand everything at once. Or perhaps ever. Finally, for all of us, there come things which cannot be understood, but only accepted.'

His voice grew harder again. 'Your being here, and continuing to be here, is one of the minor facts which can only be accepted.'

'We shan't, so there!' shouted Timmy.

'We were never your enemies,' Robert said quickly, for he had already learnt the virtues of a soft answer.

'Oh yes, you were our enemies, whether you knew it or not. Not that I hold you responsible in person — of course not, though some of my fellows, who consider me dangerously tender-minded, would not agree. . . You too — you and your people — obey the law of necessity. Unhappily there is more than one set of laws, and what is life to one is death to another. One touch of nature makes us unakin. And so the long war goes on. . .'

'What war do you mean?' Robert asked, thinking of Vietnam and Northern Ireland, those wars that had gone on for so long on television, with stones flying, guns cracking, people running this way or that, soldiers busy, and sad, slow processions with nothing to do and nowhere to go.

'No, not those petty squabbles which your world is given to, squabbles between one little party and another. But we watch your small wars with interest, for they weaken you and bring you nearer to final ruin.' It was impossible to read the expression on the Shadow's face. 'Whereas we do not fight among ourselves, since we know there is only the one true enemy, and the one true war which always continues. Never to end, some have thought, but now. . .'

Although they had heard much from their parents and their teachers about peace, and how fortunate they were to be born into it, the children had always felt vague doubts on the subject. True, they lived above ground, and not in an air-raid shelter, where their mother had spent her childhood. And if you heard a plane, you looked up to see whether it was going to crash, not whether it was going to drop bombs on you. But even so it didn't seem to them that life was exactly peaceful, if what peaceful meant was full of peace. Timmy said that peace was what happened when you were sleeping, but Robert wasn't sure about that. Was it this that the Shadow was talking about? The children weren't certain that they understood him, or wanted to.

'But I doubt that your parents will have told you anything about *that* war. Not many of you are truly conscious of it, of the war between the Dark and the Light. . . Some of your more perceptive writers have had inklings of the truth. The poet, the blind bad-tempered one, what was his name? —'

'John Milton?' Jane suggested.

'Yes, Milton. "Sable-vested Night, eldest of things". . . Very fine!' For a moment his reedy voice softened. 'He had some understanding of it, though much of the time he was standing on his head. That other poet, too — "O that this too too solid flesh would melt. . ." He knew something about it. But your people have commonly

40

dismissed such men as mere fantasts, concocters of allegories, scribblers of fairy-tales for children. . .'

After quite a lengthy silence he said harshly, 'The Light is our enemy: that is all you need to know. Ours and now yours.'

'But if you are shadows then you depend on light,' Robert said.

'Yes, perhaps, in the sense that you, though followers of Light, depend on Darkness to satisfy some of your needs and desires. But this is mere quibbling.'

'No, it's not,' persisted Robert, 'because without light you wouldn't exist at all!'

The tall Shadow became visibly angry; he seemed to grow darker and more corporeal.

'Light is the enemy. We belong to the Dark, we are a part of Darkness. Light would destroy us, wipe us out utterly. . . As utterly as we could destroy you if we wished. Or if you obliged us to.'

The children felt themselves fading, melting away into thinness, pallor and weakness.

The Shadow continued in a calmer voice. 'You say I would not exist without Light. Who can tell? There is no way of knowing. But very well – let the Light be quenched then, and I will gladly put your theory to the test, at the risk of my existence! In one sense you may be correct. To have an enemy is necessary to us – and to your people too, I would judge. Without an enemy of some kind to contend with, to measure ourselves against, perhaps none of us would last for long. . .'

There came another silence.

'But I was always given to the finer points of philosophy. It is my weakness. . . My name, by the way, is Finsterness. I should have introduced myself before.'

41

The Shadow had gone. The children sat in silence, still trembling a little, until the door opened and Lily and Leslie came in. They were escorted by a smaller Shadow, whom the children could tell was a woman, a woman Shadow. They could see, too, that the twins were less frightened and dejected, looking for the moment more solid, somehow, certainly more substantial than they themselves were feeling.

The woman Shadow came up to them, looked into their faces, and touched them gently on their shoulders before she left.

The five of them settled down and tried to make sense of what they had seen and heard, and so comfort one another.

7 · Twilight Sleep

For some time after that nothing much happened. Or what happened seemed to be happening inside them, secretly. They couldn't describe it to one another, but the twins remarked in superior fashion that *they* knew all about it, and there was more to come yet.

It was as if their senses were gradually dulling, their heart-beats slowing, the blood thickening and moving less quickly in their veins. In fact, among other things, that was what was happening. There was nothing of pain in the process, or even of physical discomfort: rather the opposite, for the senses were beginning to perceive less acutely whatever might give pain.

Robert rubbed his bare arms: it was like gooseflesh in reverse. Perhaps what people called 'twilight sleep'. He was the only one of them to feel much anxiety on this score, and he did his best to keep his feelings from the others, confining himself to putting down the twins when they grew intolerably smug. The thought crossed his mind that the twins behaved like kids in their second year at school coming it over new pupils.

How long *had* Lily and Leslie been here, he wondered? Years and years, they said, and clearly believed it. Yet for how long had they been missing? It looked as if time was another mystery in this world

43

of mysteries. And memory, too — but perhaps that was part of the same thing.

* * *

The Shadow who had introduced himself as Finsterness visited them again. He seemed faintly embarrassed, or would have seemed so had he been a human.

'I hear — I am told by the Shadow who attends to you — something of how you must be feeling. . . That it is like being in a — a mist, I think she said. Nothing holds fast, nothing is firm. You have an expression, I believe, *terra firma*. . . And nothing is quite — distinct. As if you were partially blind. . . Let me assure you that you cannot hurt yourselves — nothing can hurt you. There are no barbed-wire fences to walk into, no precipices to fall over. No lampposts' — his face wrinkled with what could have been pain or disgust — 'to bump into. You cannot be hurt — once you have accepted what it is beyond your power to deny. . . And so, you see, it is no worse than walking at ease through an innocent mist on your own lawn.'

'It is like being in prison,' said Robert.

'It *is* being in prison,' said Timmy, with all the confidence of one who was intimately acquainted with that condition.

'No sickness, no pain,' the Shadow continued as if he hadn't heard them. 'No violent death. Except in battle, and that is left mostly to the professionals. Hardly death at all, you might say. For why should a Shadow kill another Shadow? He has no reason to do so — he is free from ambition, selfishness, hatred, jealousy, he has no desire for gain, all his wants are met. . . So, if it is death you are afraid of, there is no need for you to fear.'

44

But it wasn't death the children were afraid of.

'Education, yes, or re-education. But that is nothing to fear. It won't last for very long, as time goes here. Our educational methods are highly developed, and schooling will take up no more than a minute fraction of your time — nothing like the third or quarter of the life-span that it consumes in the world you have come from. And where, so we gather, some never survive it.'

Robert thought of his old school. They were halfway through building a scale model, battery-powered, of a lighthouse. And then they were planning to tackle a whole Roman army, complete with chariots (the master told them that the chariot was said to have been invented by some chappie who was unlucky enough to have a serpent's tail for legs, which he thought best to conceal from the public gaze), and battering rams, and catapults for hurling rocks and flaming brands, and a tortoise made by overlapping shields ('testudo' the master called it). . .

Jane wanted her mother, and her father, even though he was rarely quite *there*. She wanted the house, and her room, and the little garden, which was uncared-for and didn't have anything that could be called a lawn. . .

Timmy, with the least to remember, was not very far from beginning to want nothing. Or only sleep, for the Shadow's words had tired him. But he asked Finsterness about pets. The word was incomprehensible to the Shadow.

'Cats, dogs, rabbits,' said Timmy indignantly, 'who live with you like friends.'

Ah no, there were no 'pets': the Shadows considered 'pets' a pest, a source of pollution, wastage and incontinence, and conducive to unsuitable emotionality.

Finsterness assumed that Timmy wouldn't care for a big black furry spider, would he?

'Do you have any other questions?' Finsterness asked them. Robert had lots, but he knew he must step carefully.

'No,' said Timmy loudly and in a bored voice.

'Thank you,' added Jane.

'One last thing,' said Finsterness. 'When something happens to you, often it is because you *want* it to happen — without knowing.'

8 · *Adum Brate and Others*

Every morning – after they had slept, at any rate, for otherwise they couldn't tell whether it was morning, afternoon or night – the five children were taken to a special room in the Shadeau for their lessons. Timmy thought of them as 'lessens', because he felt more insubstantial and diminished after every one.

The name of this room, painted on the door, was 'Institute of Shadoctrination', and inside it was a combination of schoolroom and cinema, with on one wall a blackboard (on which the Shadofficer in charge wrote with chalk which was hardly less black) and on another a wide black screen. Strange charts hung on the other walls, including a large photograph of what Robert guessed to be an atomic bomb exploding in Japan. This was hard to make out since the Shadows found it distressing to their sensibilities and it had been covered over with what looked like smoked glass.

Here the children were instructed in the history, beliefs and culture of their captors. The lessons were so long that they found themselves nodding off to sleep – except that they then had a dreadful sensation of falling through space, as if they were being gently licked by a large tongue and, like an ice-lolly, getting thinner and thinner. It was better to stay awake, and to pay attention,

47

even if at first they could follow little of what was taught them. It was best to show interest, and Robert in particular grew expert at asking intelligent-sounding questions, for otherwise the Shadows grew angry and turned a deeper dark, which was very frightening. At such times the children felt themselves dwindling away fast.

A Doctor of Shadosophy called Obfusc – for so he had introduced himself – taught them about the long history of the Shadows. He told them about the much venerated and much feared Primal Night who created their world in the beginning – 'Let there be Dark: and there was Dark' – and the first Shadow, Adum Brate, from whom over the centuries they had sprung, the ancestor of them all. The children learnt about the Emperor of All the Shades, about the Great Shah, and the President of the Shades, and Graf von Schatten, also known as Shaitan, a fierce and dedicated warrior.

They heard of the poet Penumbra, who wrote shadow plays and poems and was famous for his dying words: 'More dark!' One of his poems they were made to learn by heart:

> *'Dear, beauteous death, the jewel of the night,*
> *Shining nowhere but in the dark.*
> *What mysteries do lie beyond thy might,*
> *Could Shadow but outlook that mark!'*

Something else they learnt was an old song, a ballad telling of a Shadow who fell in love with a human girl and how he went over to that other country to be with her. It ended very sadly, and the children grew to like it.

They became acquainted with much else. With the Dimsday Book, a record of the lands once held by the ancient princes and nobles, many of them now lost to the Shadows. With the mighty Shadoissimo and his band of Barrens who struggled long and gallantly to preserve the Dark Ages. With Count Chimera and Prince Ténébreux and their knights, and many other heroes who fought unyieldingly against the invading Light and the gross physical shapes which the Light had engendered.

They were made to memorise the legend of the Lady Umber, who (so it went) was burnt at the stake by a savage mob of Lightists; the story of Obit, the great bishop and missionary, who (by means not dwelt on) made many converts among the heathen; the adventures of the patriotic buccaneer, Schwarzbart, and his daring attacks on lighthouses and lightships; and the life of the great healer, Schattenfreude, who had cured sick Shadows afflicted with the delusion that they were turning into three-dimensional monsters.

Speaking in reedy tones which at first the children found difficult to follow, their teachers lectured them on the Black Arts and their many beauties; on Black Friday, the anniversary of the dreadful day when their enemies had discovered electricity; on Black Stone, the stern but wise lawgiver, and the composer Chiaroscuro, famous throughout the land for his delicate nocturnes; on John Nox, the exalted divine who perfected the rituals of the Black Mass, and Saint Shadost, much revered, who fell into hostile hands, to be tortured with wax candles and then crucified on a chandelier; on the brilliant but possibly unstable philosopher, Nightshade, and his doctrine of the Supershadow, the Will to Night, and Eternal Darkness; on Crepuscule, the educational pioneer, whose methods they were now benefiting from. . .

They were also told, with grim emphasis, about the Black Baskervilles, a fearsome breed of hounds used for tracking down and recapturing escaped Lightists.

From the strange films they were shown they learnt rather less, often failing to satisfy the leading questions of their instructors, who always wore dark glasses and stern expressions on these occasions. The images were dim and erratic, flickering like the old movies they had watched on television long before. The purpose of the films — so much they could understand — was to demonstrate the superiority of the Shadows and their way of life. The Shadows were always wise and brave and considerate and self-sacrificing, whereas their enemies, the Lightists, were shown only as white blanks edged with red — ungainly, brutal, foolish, self-seeking, flaring up violently like sunspots or exploding stars, breaking things, falling about, maiming and destroying themselves and others.

At other times the children were forced to sit and watch a shadocast series concerning the simple joys and sorrows of ordinary Shadow citizens. Mostly they couldn't distinguish the joys from the sorrows, and found it long-drawn-out and lifeless. There was also a historical series in progress, each episode lasting five hours, which pictured the Endarkenment and its social and intellectual achievements, all quite colourless and much of it incomprehensible to them.

'At least in *our* history people wear funny clothes,' Timmy grumbled.

There was something else they learnt by heart — that there was a place, much more horrible than anything they had seen so far, called the Black Hole. That was where bad children went to — or, as the Shadows put it when they were angry with them, it was a place of visible darkness, a pit of black flames, prepared for those who refused to cooperate.

The children were so exhausted after these sessions that they fell asleep without eating.

9 · *A Bright Idea*

One day Timmy had a bright idea. It must be admitted that it grew out of discontent and waywardness rather than bravery, but at least it grew.

The children were at their lessons, watching an educational film about the wild life of the Black Forest. It was extremely tame.

It was also very long, because the reel of film unwound so slowly. Then Timmy had his idea. If he dislodged the film projector, it would crash to the ground and explode in a great flash of light. That, he knew, was what film projectors did. And this, he told himself, would surely knock out the Shadow teacher and his assistant, maybe doing them untold damage, and then the children could run away. If it did nothing else, it would put an end to this dull, endless filmshow.

Timmy hadn't forgotten the warnings about the Black Hole, but he reckoned that it couldn't be much blacker than the Black Forest.

Cautiously he shifted his seat nearer to the table on which the projector stood. The Shadows were apparently fascinated by the film, the teacher telling the assistant how he had spent a holiday in the northern province, walking in the Black Forest. Timmy jabbed swiftly at the projector with his elbow.

52

It didn't budge. It was like the time he had tried to punch Leslie in the head. His elbow melted into the projector.

But there must be a way, Timmy reasoned. If the projector could be carried, it could be dropped, and if it stood on the table, then surely it could be persuaded to fall off the table?

He thought a little more. And in so doing he discovered the principle of the lever. True, Archimedes had discovered it some while before, but Timmy hadn't heard of Archimedes.

As his lever he made use of the ruler provided to further his education, and as the fulcrum he chose the edge of the table. Stealthily he pushed one end of the ruler between the legs of the projector and under its base, and then pressed down on its other end, slowly increasing his weight. He felt resistance, and he saw the projector tilting.

Out of the corner of his eye he glimpsed Robert shaking his head urgently. But then the projector toppled off the table.

There came a muted explosion, and a blinding flash.

It wasn't the flash of light Timmy had expected, but a great flash of darkness. And it threw him on his back. He felt as though an immense vacuum cleaner was sucking the life out of him, and he lost consciousness.

*   *   *

When Timmy came round, a few long seconds later, the Shadows were arguing in consternation and alarm. How, they were asking, had this expensive piece of apparatus come to fall? Or was it pushed?

'It is not in the nature of film projectors to move

53

of their own accord,' said the teacher severely.

'It's those children!' grumbled the janitor, as he cleaned up the remains. 'Clumsy little beasts. Should be sent back where they came from!'

'*Naturally* clumsy, being what they are,' the teacher corrected him coldly. 'Now you see what we educational experts are up against!' He didn't like that sort of loose talk from an inferior.

Robert was leaning over Timmy, helping him to his feet. 'Next time you have an idea, tell me first,' he hissed. He didn't know whether to be furious with his young brother or proud of him.

Once they had recovered from the shock of this unseemly occurrence, the Shadows showed themselves quite solicitous, and insisted on feeling Timmy all over for broken bones. They were relieved to find none, for shock treatment was frowned on at this stage, and however badly the child might have behaved, they would be in trouble had he come to serious harm.

The woman Shadow had been sent for. She took Timmy by the arm and led him away. He had better lie down for a while.

'I want Jane,' he said in his most pathetic voice, and so Jane was allowed to go with him.

The teacher didn't think it worthwhile continuing the lesson for Robert alone. To tell the truth, he rather felt like lying down himself. So Robert returned to their room with the others.

As soon as the woman Shadow had left, assuring them that there was no need to worry, Robert gave his brother a good talking-to, and so did Jane.

10 · *Shadow Boxing*

'All play and no work makes Jack fit to shirk,' announced Finsterness. 'That is one of your sayings, isn't it?'

'No,' said Robert, adding in a flash of inspiration, 'But this is — The night cometh when no man can work!'

The Shadow winced, or perhaps grinned painfully. 'We do not have many sports — nothing like as many as your people — because there is little of the competitive instinct here. . . But you have been working quite hard, and if you would care for solo chess, or demon patience, or blackgammon, or crossword puzzles, or ombre — which I gather used to be popular among Lightists of the politer classes — or tiddly-winks, then we can accommodate you. Or even clock-golf, though that's rather slow and it takes a year or more to finish a match.'

The children looked so glum that he grinned again, this time unmistakably. It struck Robert that the Shadow was actually being playful.

'Let's see what else we can offer.' He beckoned to them to follow him outside.

'Look,' he said proudly, holding up what they supposed must be his idea of a football. 'Let's see if you can — what did you say? — dribble with this.'

The children had a kick-about, but it wasn't awfully satisfactory, since either their feet sank so far into the

55

ball that it didn't move or else it shot off at such speed that they couldn't follow its flight. Timmy noticed one minor advantage: when he fell, as he often did, he only felt a faint sensation of dizziness.

Finsterness's attempts at staging a cricket match didn't work either, since most of the time the ball simply passed right through the bat. And sometimes through the stumps as well.

'The light is failing, as we say,' remarked Robert, causing Finsterness some quiet amusement.

Then they tried shadow boxing, and this was much more successful. Except that Leslie turned out to be so much better at it than anyone else.

'Over-development of the assertive ego,' Finsterness tut-tutted. 'Quite typical.'

Timmy agreed. 'Big head,' he muttered under his breath.

Finsterness threw up his hands, rather alarmingly. 'Oh well, you'll have to do without "sport", as we do. But later on, when you've — adjusted to our conditions, I shall take you to ride our Shadow horses. They're as fleet as the wind.'

Jane thought that sounded most agreeable. It was something to look forward to.

11 · *Prisoners*

The Lacey twins had told them that the woman Shadow who now looked after them most of the time was called Sable, and she was the nicest of them all. Indeed, Sable showed warmth towards them, and Jane in particular grew fond of her as the days and nights went past. Once she found herself on the point of calling Sable 'Mummy' — and when she thought of this, she cried with longing and with fear, a mixture of feelings that she couldn't sort out.

'Why can't we all live together?' Sable said once, as if arguing with herself. 'Or live separately, which is much the same thing — live and let live? Why must the long war go on between my people and yours?'

The children said nothing, for they had nothing to say.

'There is Light enough for those who desire it. And Darkness enough for those who live by it. Are we each of us afraid of the other, or is each driven to try to change the other? To re-create him in our own image? I suppose everybody fears the thing that is different, and fear turns to hate.'

'That's right,' confirmed Timmy, and went on to a long boring story about some other little boy at school whom he just couldn't get on with, and how they had a fight in the playground, but some busybody of a grown-up came along and dragged them apart, and after that they were rather friendly, because. . .

Robert put his hand over Timmy's mouth. He wanted to hear whatever else Sable might say. Who could tell? — it might help them to escape one day.

'We are all prisoners,' said Sable sadly, as if she had read his thoughts. 'There's no escape. We are prisoners of the past, and the past creates our future. None of us can break away and start afresh.'

Jane took her hand. 'I'm not your enemy,' she said.

*   *   *

One day, when Sable took the five of them for a walk through the dim cobwebby woods which lay to the south of the Shadeau, she was almost gay.

'There aren't any *colours*. I'm bored,' said Timmy ungratefully. 'But not as bored as I was.'

Robert had noticed that he too was not so conscious of boredom, or of fear, as he had been earlier in their stay. The realization worried him, for he had heard of people growing used to captivity, and finally content with it. Happiness wasn't replacing fear or boredom, though, and he felt sure it never would.

'Soon you will have a special treat,' Sable told them. 'A party, a feast, a little excitement,' she added rather wistfully.

She told them, with some shyness, that before long she was to be married.

'To Finsterness?' asked Jane hopefully.

Yes, to Finsterness. And there would be a wedding reception, to which she was inviting them. Some of the Shadows considered it too early for the children to be given the freedom of social life, but she had insisted —

58

and Finsterness was on her side. Since Finsterness was a notability — a Very Important Shadow, you could say — it had been settled that they should attend. Though of course they would have to be on their best behaviour. In a way it was a coming-out party for them, marking the end of the first stage of their life in the country.

Robert kicked at a large stone, and as usual his foot merged into it and then merged out. He was disturbed by Sable's words: 'the end of the first stage' meant the beginning of the second.

But Jane was hopping with happiness. 'I do think Finsterness is nice.'

'As they go,' mumbled Robert.

Timmy was chasing a black butterfly, and wondering vaguely how he could see it if it was really black. 'Come on, Leslie,' he shouted. 'Let's see who can fall into the most ditches.'

'So you have marriage here too,' Robert said, trying to chase away the black thoughts that had settled on him.

'I'm sure you'll have a beautiful baby before long,' Jane promised.

'We have marriage,' Sable replied, 'just like you — or they — do. But,' and sorrow came into her voice, 'we don't have babies.'

Shadows, she explained, couldn't have babies. Or didn't. The race was barren. Perhaps it had always been so: the historians were divided on the subject, some believing that Adum Brate, the first Shadow, had accidentally been exposed to the rays of the sun and thus rendered incapable of procreating, and others that it had happened later, a calamity which followed the Lightists' discovery of fire. Yet others held the opinion that it was innate and prescribed by a law of Shadow nature.

59

'But how. . .' Jane began to ask.

'We live a very long time, remember, much longer than you — than humans, I mean. And then — why do you think you were brought here? To replace the children we cannot have. . . Didn't you guess?'

Jane felt so sorry for the Shadows and their childlessness that her own grief receded further. There were so many children back at home — and some of them unwanted — that surely a few could be spared? Did it have to be them, though? Again she couldn't understand the mixture of feelings inside her.

'Oh Sable, how sad!' was all she could think of to say. 'But children aren't everything, and I know you'll be very happy with Finsterness.' Perhaps, she thought, they would adopt her — and the others, of course — and then they could all live together, in a proper home, like a proper family. That would be lovely. Then she felt a twinge of shame. She had been unfaithful.

Robert scowled, and tried longingly to stub his toe on another rock. Timmy hadn't the least interest in this talk of marrying and babies, and he was stalking a handsome and unconcerned blackbird. The twins were quarrelling in a relatively amicable fashion about which of them had been born first.

12 · *Spots on the Brain*

And so time passed.

Day and night. (For now the children were able to tell the difference between the one and the other.) Working and playing. Eating and sleeping. Remembering and forgetting.

Robert saw that they were growing away from one another, little by little. But perhaps growing away was only a part of growing up, of becoming persons. With principles and policies and points of view. Or prejudices and foibles and — an expression he had once heard somewhere — spots on the brain.

Yet the children remained good friends, in their old ways. Indeed, at the same time as they were growing apart, they were growing into something like a family, casual and unthinking. And that, Robert knew, was largely due to Sable, for without her they would have had nothing resembling a mother. Part of him resented her for that. After all, she was one of Them, one of the enemy.

*   *   *

With Sable's help Lily had made herself a collection of dolls to play with. The dolls were all grown up — there were no babies among them — and all female. And they

61

were all dressed in professional garb of one sort or another. There was a woman policeman — 'a police-woman,' Lily pointed out — and a woman doctor, a woman teacher and a woman footballer, a woman soldier and a woman sailor, a woman novelist and a woman dustman ('a dustwoman,' Lily insisted), a woman judge and a woman jury.

'Where's the woman cook and the woman washer?' mocked Leslie, but he only got a dirty look in answer.

'Where are all the babies?' Jane asked, but she received no answer at all.

Women didn't need men, Lily declared. They could be whatever they wanted to be, they could do everything, all by themselves. Nobody needed men. Men were old-fashioned.

'I'd like to help her make a man doll, for a change,' Sable whispered to Jane. 'But she won't have it. It's just a phase she's going through.'

'You're old-fashioned too,' said Lily, who had over-heard.

'But what about babies?' Jane insisted, wondering how much Lily knew about biology. 'I mean, if there aren't any men. . .'

'We shall see about babies later,' said Lily authorita-tively. First she intended to get rid of the men and make a world fit for women to live in.

Sable and Jane crept away, feeling slightly ashamed of themselves though they couldn't imagine why.

*   *   *

'I'm going to be a working man when I'm older,' said Timmy, as they ran about kicking a make-believe foot-ball into make-believe nets and scoring an enormous

62

number of goals. 'And maybe I'll be a shop-stewed too.'

'You must have lost your marbles,' Leslie said. 'There's no future in *that*. It's prac'ly finished already. Now me, I'm going to be a business boss — executioner, they call them — with a private car park and a sektry bird to make coffee and write all my letters. . . I don't like writing letters. I shall make top-level 'cisions. . . Hey, I've scored twenty-nine more goals than you!'

'I haven't been counting,' said Timmy in a superior voice, scoring another thirty in rapid succession.

'This is a silly game anyway,' Leslie said a little later. 'I'm going inside to read a good book.'

It passed through his mind that perhaps they didn't have business executioners here. And Timmy was wondering whether the Shadows went in for shop-steweds.

'I'm going inside too, to read a *better* book,' he said.

*   *   *

Robert was out in the grounds of the Shadeau, walking by himself and thinking. Not really by himself, though. He couldn't go very far without coming across a Shadow guard, tall and austere figures who pretended not to see him.

And there were others, barely noticeable, who followed him at a discreet distance. This lot are jolly good at shadowing people, he thought. He giggled childishly, causing a startled Shadow to pop out from behind a tree.

13 · Secret Agents

'Funny that their father hasn't reported the loss of his loved little ones,' Inspector Barlow remarked grumpily.

'He's a writer,' said Herr Brush, as if that were quite sufficient explanation.

'I have observed that such individuals tend to live in a world of their own,' said Mr Spock. 'Which no doubt is more convenient, for as long as it lasts.'

The three were sitting comfortlessly in the Inspector's comfortable sitting-room, the walls of which were largely covered with framed photographs of the Inspector's nieces and nephews and their offspring. Mr Spock perceived with interest that the subjects thus portrayed were of all colours and shades of colour. He wondered whether there was one with pointed ears among them.

The Inspector was well into his fourth cup of tea. Herr Brush was halfway through his second. Mr Spock was still sipping cautiously at his first. There was a pile of dried-up curling sandwiches, assorted, which none of them fancied.

The three were in despair, or nearly. Actually Mr Spock didn't know what despair was: it was not a state of mind enjoyed or otherwise by his kind. In the case of the Inspector, so many emotions were battling for possession of his face that despair could hardly hope to emerge sole victor. At the moment anger and disgust were in the ascendancy, though threatened by the satisfaction deriving from tea-drinking.

As for Herr Brush, who had torn his knickerbockers and muddied his cloak, there was too much lovingness in his nature for despair to prevail for long.

*   *   *

'Five at one fell swoop!' Inspector Barlow groaned. 'How am I going to explain it to my superiors, eh? My job isn't worth the paper it's written on. "Suffer the little children to come unto me, and forbid them not." Why, it's – it's not *Christian*!'

'I fail to follow your reasoning,' said Mr Spock, who wasn't either. 'It appears to be entirely devoid of logic.'

He placed his hand affectionately on Herr Brush's shoulder, for he was well aware that every time an incident of this kind occurred, his friend was reminded of an old sorrow of his own.

All Herr Brush said was 'My feet hurt.'

'We've checked all the known entry-points,' the Inspector said heavily. 'No signs, overt or covert, of any crossings whatsoever.'

'There may be unknown entry-points,' said Herr Brush.

'Which is something we simply don't know,' Mr Spock said.

*   *   *

They were staring at a large map of the district spread out on the Inspector's so-called coffee-table. Mr Spock was looking at it upside-down, but this didn't inconvenience him in the least.

'If only you could see in the Dark as well,' said Herr Brush plaintively.

Mrs Barlow came tiptoeing in, her plump finger to her lips, carrying a fresh pot of tea. She was a woman of generous proportions, and a good police wife. Having exchanged pots, she went out of the room on tiptoe, her finger still to her lips.

'If only we could think up some new methods, some new techniques,' the Inspector remarked longingly. 'Surely there must be something new under the sun!'

'For how many centuries have we been saying that?' Herr Brush asked. 'Even though it's not exactly the sun we're concerned with, or under the sun.'

The Inspector was toying lovingly with an illustrated catalogue of secret agent's impedimenta which he had on his lap.

'Just you look at this and see how well our colleagues in the junior branch are catered for!'

He read out descriptions of some of the items as advertised:

a cigarette lighter which took photographs, fired bullets, picked up conversations taking place within a hundred yards, and even lit cigarettes, sometimes;

a fountain pen which wrote a disguised hand in invisible ink;

a bugging device in the shape of a scarab, to be left casually on the dressing-tables of beautiful women or in equally suspect museums of Egyptology;

a vacuum cleaner designed for use in the corridors of foreign Embassies, with a bag large enough to accommodate a dwarf spy;

an innocent-looking pea-shooter which emitted signals in Morse code when blown through in the correct manner;

a pair of spectacles enabling the wearer to see what was going on behind his back, but not what was happening in front;

a false moustache which actually grew, and eventually turned grey;

a butcher's chopper which converted to a very small stiletto when a concealed button was pressed;

an electric toothbrush which knocked all the user's teeth out, thus disconcerting him;

a key which melted as soon as it was inserted in the correct lock;

a bullet-proof edition of *Hymns Ancient and Modern,* for protection in hostile churches, which played a few bars of 'Rock of ages, cleft for me' when struck sharply;

a phrase-book giving the equivalent of 'I will without delay tell all I know' in all the world's major languages and a selection of the minor ones;

and many other pieces of equipment described as 'Essential for the Agent who has Everything'.

Mr Spock wore the expression of a very patient man whose patience has been very sorely tried.

'My dear Inspector, ours is obviously a field of endeavour in which new techniques cannot make the slightest contribution. Man's spiritual nature − in as far as I am able to understand it − has not changed appreciably since the moment when some eccentric concatenation of powerful irrationalities first brought it into existence.' He smiled drily. 'Therefore the nature of the problem to which we have devoted our waking hours' − he himself never slept, or so he gave his colleagues to understand − 'has not changed appreciably either. Technological advances, gimmicks and gadgets − I fear the Inspector has been reading too much lurid fiction −'

'Fact!' bellowed the Inspector indignantly. 'Fact, not fiction! Look, there's the address to write to for free samples.'

'Somewhere in Soho, I note. . . In this sphere, my dear Inspector, your facts are as far from the truth of the matter as any fiction could be, perhaps a little further. . . As I was saying, technological advances belong to an utterly disparate conceptual category, to a dimension of thinking and being which is totally incommensurable. . .'

'Oh, you mean they won't work,' said the Inspector, throwing the catalogue into the coal scuttle.

'If however you can bring to my attention a *spiritual* advance, however modest, then I shall do my best to suggest a new spiritual technique. . .'

Once upon a time-unit, long ago, someone had told Mr Spock that he had a mind like a rapier. He was sufficiently curious to find out what a rapier was — it was a typically uncouth (not to say nasty) Earth weapon, a length of sharp pointed metal used for interfering with the patient work of tissue, protoplasm, plasma and corpuscles. Sober and unmalicious though Mr Spock was, occasionally he couldn't deny himself the curious pleasure of needling his less sharp friends.

'I am only a humble police officer, as it were,' Inspector Barlow informed the world, not for the first time. 'I never passed through Police College, oh no, not Barlow, I worked my way up from the taxi-ranks.' He paused for these regrettable considerations to sink in. 'I am merely a little finger of the Law — whatever I am, I am *not* a spiritualist, oh no.'

Mr Spock glanced at the Inspector's handsome mahogany bookcase. True, there were some highly suspicious paperbacks on the lower shelves, but the upper were

68

packed with solidly bound volumes on Law, Criminology, Ancient Myth and Religion, The Psychology of the Child-Snatcher, and Black Magic (with a Supplement on Other Shades). Mr Spock raised his eyebrows.

'In any case,' Herr Brush pointed out consolingly, 'even if we did improve ourselves by getting cleverer, then they would improve themselves by getting cleverer too — and we'd only be back where we started.'

'So it's very simple,' the Inspector said, disgruntled. 'We are completely in the dark.'

'*They* are in the Dark,' Herr Brush said quietly. 'The children. It depends on them, doesn't it, more than on us... It always has.' Absent-mindedly he took a sandwich.

'*Ad augusta per angusta*,' remarked Mr Spock. 'Or, as the French say, I believe, the most beautiful girl in the world cannot give more than she has.'

'*I* fail to see any logic in what *you* are saying!' shouted the Inspector. 'Beautiful girls, eh? I shall have to keep an eye on you.'

'And time is running out so fast,' said Herr Brush, beginning to choke.

'Have another cup of tea,' the Inspector advised. 'Then we'll go back on patrol.'

14 · *Flight!*

Finsterness proved as good as his word. If the children wanted to go out riding, then they could. Horses were at their disposal.

'Let's see the horses first,' said Timmy.

They were unlike 'human horses', Finsterness told them, in that they never fell, but simply soared through obstacles. The children might fall off them, of course, but no bones would be broken. And the horses, though very fast, were by nature and training docile and easy to recapture.

Even so, Lily and Leslie declined to get on the back of the tall, long-necked and slender-legged animals. 'We wouldn't want,' said Lily, 'to *break* them,' said Leslie piously.

Finsterness assured them that stone walls wouldn't break those horses, so they need have no fear. He offered to give them a hand up.

'Who do you think we are?' asked Lily and Leslie in plangent harmony, as they retreated. 'Harvey Smith?' asked Leslie. 'Princess Anne?' asked Lily.

'I like fat silky cows better,' Lily added. 'Fat silky bulls,' Leslie amended the statement.

For once Timmy was of the same mind as the twins, if for different reasons (he didn't care for cows or bulls either), and thought it no disgrace to deny himself what Finsterness obviously considered a great privilege.

Jane had once attended a riding school — paid for by Granny — and she was enthusiastic, especially as Sable promised to ride with her.

Robert too professed enthusiasm, cautiously: he had something different in mind.

*   *   *

Robert's horse, a handsome creature, was called Wolken. Robert felt quite proud as he sat high up on its slim back.

'Remember, Wolken flies very fast, but you needn't be afraid,' Finsterness had said as he handed over the reins. 'He doesn't bolt, he knows what he is doing. Wolken follows his nature.'

Perhaps that made riding him all too easy, thought Robert: but why should he complain of that, he didn't want to break his own neck, did he?

The horses trotted gently along a narrow path, through sparse woods, until they came to open country. Sable and Jane, who was on a mare called Nubila, were chatting, Sable keeping a needlessly solicitous eye on her young charge.

'Don't ride too far!' she called out to Robert.

Timmy was playing with the twins somewhere. He had become quite an admirer of Leslie, who was training him in the art of shadow boxing. It struck Robert that he himself was the odd man out now — the unforgiving one, the unforgetting one.

*   *   *

Out there, in the open, it needed only a light pressure

71

of the heels and the horse, as Finsterness had put it, followed his nature. Robert found that Wolken was very easy to control: a mere hint of a pull on the rein, and the horse changed course at once. And what a speed he had! Finsterness had used the right word: Wolken didn't gallop, he flew. The landscape flickered past indistinctly. Before long Robert was out of sight of his sister and Sable, out of sight of everyone, on his own. He passed a black cow, chewing the cud, that was all.

He had no idea of which direction he should take, except that it must lead him away from the Shadeau. Eventually — and at Wolken's speed eventually should arrive fairly soon — he ought to find himself, if not home, then on the way there.

He felt no fear, only elation. A feeling stronger and more precise than any he had known for a long time. A prisoner's duty, so he had gathered from some dimly recollected television programme about a prisoner-of-war camp in Germany, was to escape, at least to try to. There was no possibility of taking the others with him, so he would have to leave them. For the present, at all events.

Wolken seemed tireless. There was no telling how many miles they had covered already; nor, of course, how many more they had to cover still. Hours had gone by, and the motion of the animal was so smooth and regular — not once had the rider come near to falling off — that Robert felt himself growing drowsy.

The countryside was flat and monotonous. No hills, no valleys, no rivers or pools, just a few vague trees, no signs of habitation, only a vague black cow chewing the cud. . .

It was all too easy. He must keep a sharp look-out.

Letting the reins fall, he pinched his thigh. The horse flew even faster.

*   *   *

Robert had nodded off for a moment. Recovering himself with a start, he saw a figure on a stationary horse, not fifty yards ahead of him.

It was Finsterness, sitting there coolly. He spoke a word, and Wolken stopped dead in his flight, throwing Robert clean over his head.

'Oh dear,' said Finsterness softly. 'It was a little too soon for you to be riding out alone, wasn't it?'

Robert scrambled back on the horse and urged him on. But Wolken failed to respond: he stood there like a statue.

'And so it falls to me to save you from yourself. From your old self.'

'My self is still my self,' said Robert, hoping he sounded defiant and not merely petulant.

'You are trying to resist the irresistible. . . But very well, I am saving you from the highly unpleasant consequences – believe me – of a vain attempt to run away. . .'

Another word from Finsterness, and Wolken turned about. The two horses cantered side by side, back towards the Shadeau.

'You are – playing with fire. Yes, that idiom is apt enough,' Finsterness said between his teeth. 'And perhaps I should have left you to get burnt. A burnt child. . . There are some who whisper that I am what they contemptuously term a "humanist". . . Possibly they are right.'

Clearly Finsterness was angry and upset, and not a further word passed between them.

Robert felt angry, too, but also foolish. In a very short time, although the horses were not moving fast, they had caught up with Sable and Jane, who waved casually to them. All those many miles he had fled towards freedom! — compressed into a few short minutes of gentle trotting. He had got nowhere.

15·*Black Moon*

Perhaps this was peace, Robert mused, this state of mind, this remote feeling that was almost no feeling at all.

It was less dark than usual, a soft twilight, and the almost invisible birds were twittering spectrally.

Robert had been aware of a gradual blunting of his senses during the time spent here, but perhaps – it now occurred to him – perhaps it was the outside, the sounds and sights and smells, that were less vivid – or less violent – than of old. For now, he realized, his hearing was sensitive enough to detect the tiny noises made by the shy animals going about their invisible business in the obscure undergrowth of hedges and banks.

The trees spread almost down to the sea, the famous Black Sea (not that Black Sea he could recall having heard about in a previous life), with just a band of fine black sand between.

It was dreamlike, Jane had commented, and it struck Robert that he had not dreamt once since that first night. Nor had the others, they said.

'I used to have silly dreams once,' said Lily sternly, 'of fighting and shooting and killing,' added Leslie with simple relish. 'I was getting married in a church, with lots of babies round me all pretending they were mine,' Lily continued disgustedly, 'and sometimes I was a

75

cowboy and sometimes a Nindian, or a Namerican bang-banging at Japs, or a jungly Jap with a big curvy sword,' Leslie said excitedly.

'What are *dreams*?' Sable enquired.

'What you do when you're not doing anything, of course,' said Timmy scornfully.

'It's when you're asleep, but not quite,' Robert told her, 'and you go on living — but very strange lives. Impossible things happen — oh and possible ones too, but you probably wouldn't actually do them if you were awake. . . Sometimes dreams are nice, but not often. Perhaps what is happening to us now is just a dream.' Not that he thought it was.

Timmy and Leslie started a silly squabble about each of them not wanting the other to mess about in *his* dreams, thank you.

'No, this is no dream!' said Sable. 'Don't think that.' The Shadows never dreamt, she told them. Dreams, she supposed, were for short-lived races who had to make the most of their time. Also, she thought to herself, for rash and violent beings who had to get up to something destructive even when they were meant to be sleeping.

'We need dreams,' said Robert. He had heard a little about the subject at school, his other school. 'To clean out our minds. So our system doesn't get blocked up.' He added vaguely, 'Or else our brains would burst, like a frozen pipe.'

'For us one life is sufficient,' Sable said. But it was far too peaceful for them to want to argue. And Sable had something else on her mind.

* * *

They had just finished their picnic lunch. Lily and

76

Leslie were building a sandcastle, their Shadeau they called it. Timmy was wandering about in search of coal-black sea-shells. If he could find them here, thought Robert, then his eyes must have changed considerably. Perhaps they had.

Jane of course was lying near Sable, her head in the other's lap. She was humming the ballad they had learnt, about the Shadow who fell in love with a human girl. It told how the Shadow visited his sweetheart only at night, concealing himself during the day in the dark caves of that foreign land or in thickets where the sun couldn't penetrate. But the girl's brothers lay in wait for him and surrounded him with blazing torches, so that he was trapped and he gave up the ghost in agony. The girl, or so the ballad left one to suppose, died in the burning house.

Yes, Robert reflected, Sable is kind. She really does care for us. She feels. She's different somehow from the other ones, even Finsterness. Why is that? — in a place where there are no differences between people, no separateness, and all feelings are supposed to be shared? And yet there must be feelings of one's own, personal ones — even if he, Robert, couldn't make them out. For Sable was going to marry Finsterness, and surely she had feelings for him which she couldn't share, and wouldn't want to.

It was so hard to understand. . . Perhaps he would come not to want to understand. Just to *be* — if this was what be-ing was to be for them now. Perhaps he would grow to accept — that was what Finsterness had said, once he had recovered his composure after Robert's attempted escape. 'The ones that are hardest to win over are the ones most worth winning,' he had remarked in a fairly amiable manner.

But Robert didn't want that, he didn't want it, not yet. He must find out more about the Shadows, the Shadeau, the land, everything he possibly could – and Sable was the only one from whom he might learn.

*   *   *

Jane was begging Sable to tell her what was troubling her. Something was wrong, she knew. And just when Sable was about to be married: *that,* she added in adult tones, was not the time to worry, only before and after.

Sable murmured that it was nothing really. . . nothing more than nerves. . . her wedding-dress didn't quite fit. . . and the party. . . lots of people scared her. . .

'Who?' demanded Jane.

A crowded room of people, she meant. . . It was nothing really. . .

No one was convinced.

'Tell us a story, Sable,' Timmy asked, feeling that there was one in the vicinity.

At last, after Robert too had lent his persuasions, Sable told them.

Sable was in love with Finsterness, who had been good to her when – well, in her early years – and Finsterness, she believed, loved her. Perhaps a little less than she loved him, for that was in the nature of things, and some things couldn't be changed.

They thought this sounded terribly sad and romantic, but what it meant they weren't at all sure. So Jane made noises of a vaguely sympathetic and encouraging sort.

'That sounds like what our mum always says,' commented Lily disapprovingly. 'It's always the woman that pays,' added Leslie knowingly.

But there was someone else who wanted Sable, and she was afraid of what he might do, late though it was. A person whose power in the government of the Shadeau was equal to Finsterness's, but twisted and cruel and vindictive. His name was Hecatus, Sable told the children, and in secret he was known as 'Black Moon' by those who feared him. He had pursued her for many years, despite the fear and dislike which he knew she felt for him, and despite her long understanding with Finsterness — 'engagement, you would say' — and all Finsterness's reasoning had failed to dissuade or discourage him.

The Shadows lived in quiet amity, for the greater part, and jealous strife of this nature was virtually unknown among them. It had already caused alarm and dissension in the highest circles, and ordinary Shadows were nervous lest it should lead to a greater split, affecting public matters. Their fear of invasion, of the enemy outside, made them very sensitive to the behaviour, real or rumoured, of officials who stood high in the service of the state.

Sable was full of guilt at being the cause of this bitterness and anxiety — but worse, she was terrified of what Hecatus might yet do. Of late he had gone out of his way to profess friendliness for Finsterness, but she was sure he hadn't changed in his feelings.

'That's a good story,' said Timmy. 'I want to hear the ending.'

'Black!' cried Lily, 'Moon!' cried Leslie. And they shuddered in unison. Soon after they had arrived there had been an unhappy incident. They hadn't liked school at the best of times, and the difficult and boring lessons on Shadow history made them so miserable and sick that one day they tore up their books — 'we must have been strong in those days,' Leslie remarked wistfully — and threw the fragments over a Shadow who happened to be passing by. It was 'Black Moon', and his fury was extreme and terrifying.

'You were so scared that you practically faded out of sight,' Leslie said. 'So did you!' Lily retorted. 'Well, if one twin disappears, then the other must as well. Can't have one twin only, it stands to reason.' 'Boy twins shouldn't be allowed,' said Lily, '*that's* what stands to reason!'

When peace had been restored, the twins went on to tell how it was Sable who had interceded for them and calmed the angry Shadow down. That was how they first came to know her.

To Jane, Sable's story was even more romantic now. 'Just think, Sable, there are *two* men — two Shadows — in love with you!'

To Robert there seemed something wrong about the story. 'We've been taught that Shadows never fight with other Shadows, that they live in peace and quietness and understanding, unlike the people we come from. So why do you worry so much about this — this person and what he might do? He can't do very much. . .'

But there was something Sable hadn't told them. A secret which she wasn't meant to disclose to them. Something which the Shadows never mentioned, which most of them didn't know about. But alas Hecatus did know — and that was the cause of all the trouble.

Yes, she would tell them. What harm could it do? It might even make them feel less unhappy — more at home, even.

She explained that she too had been a stolen child —

like them. Oh, it was many years ago. She couldn't recall her first world at all, except for her brother, whom she had loved dearly and would never forget. Not even the town she had lived in then, not even the country.

Like them, she had been miserable and rebellious at first. She tried to escape, she refused to answer the Shadow teachers, she attempted to starve herself to death but only found that she was turning into a Shadow all the faster. There were no other children about at the time. She closed her lips together tight and spoke to no one, she was forgetting how to speak.

Then, as the days passed, silent and lonely, she became aware of a special Shadow, not anonymous like the others, a young Shadow called Finsterness, who was kind to her, as kindness went among Shadows. Young, as she later realized, for he seemed old to her then, and shy, he brought her delicacies to eat. Though she wouldn't touch them. And he talked to her, held lengthy conversations — 'for a long time they were monologues, but I know now that he was reading my thoughts, so really they were conversations.'

As time went by she came to distinguish between one Shadow and another, between the kind-hearted and the stern. Gradually, for all her resistance, she began to forget the past, except for her brother, and to accept her fate. Her life was there because it could be nowhere else. She became a Shadow, like the other Shadows. Many of them too, the newcomers, the ones who were not ancient and original Shadows, must have started as humans, like her, like Lily and Leslie, and Robert and Jane and Timmy. But no one talked about such things, no one thought about them. Except Hecatus.

'It seems strange to you that two men — two Shadows

81

– should fight over me, doesn't it? That's what Robert meant –'

'I didn't mean it that way,' Robert said gruffly. 'Only that people's feelings here are like their bodies and everything else – sort of quietened down, or muffled. Not strong and noisy, like –'

'Yes, the passions of Shadows are shadowy – and, you know, I wouldn't have it otherwise. But there are exceptions, whatever they may tell you in the Dunkel-kammer. . . You see, Hecatus dearly wishes to father a child, a child of his own – this desire is stronger in him even than his political ambitions, which are uncommonly strong for a Shadow. Yet possibly they are one and the same – to father a child would increase his power enor-mously, and his popularity, which is sadly lacking at the moment. . .'

'But you said that Shadows couldn't have children,' Jane objected.

'There are many legends that say the opposite, old wives' tales, perhaps, or old husbands', and many peo-ple who do believe it is possible for a Shadow to father a child, in certain circumstances. . .'

Robert could guess what the circumstances were: he had noticed that the Shadows with whom they had most contact seemed more interested in Jane and Lily than in the three boys. Perhaps political ambitions were not so rare among Shadows as Sable believed.

'That is, if the woman is – if she was stolen from the human world, from the Lightists – and if she still keeps the memory of her family fresh. As I still remember my brother – which is something else that Hecatus knows. . .'

'Does Finsterness want a baby, too?' Jane asked.

'He smiles at the stories, and says there are enough Shadows already. . . No, Finsterness is fond of me for my own sake. While Hecatus only wants me as a means of fulfilling his ambitions, as a tool. And if I failed him . . .'

She rose and, with the five children round her, walked slowly back towards the Shadeau, shimmering softly in the deepening shades.

16 · A Famous Victory

It was a special festival. Something called the Festival of Night. Finsterness suggested that Sable should take the children to watch the — 'the festivities'. The ghost of a grin that crept over his face reminded Robert vaguely of somebody he had once met. A Mr Spick, was it, or Span?

It would be a change from lessons, the children supposed: even though Finsterness had made a grimmish reference to the 'informative value' of the outing.

Finsterness himself wasn't able to go with them, because of a high-level conference of political and military leaders, and Sable was unhappy about this. Some of the more militant Shadows — 'eagles' they were nicknamed — were of the opinion that the country was growing soft and flabby, that its national identity, its natural momentum and destined purpose, were threatened by the laxity, miscalled 'liberalism', of certain senior officials. Among these latter, as he knew, and as Sable knew, was Finsterness. For he was by nature — what a tricky word that is! — a conservative rather than an expansionist, and believed in strengthening the country by guile and watchfulness rather than force of arms.

Finsterness reckoned that moderate counsels would prevail, but the balance of power, not only between his world and the other but also within the government of his world, was delicately poised. The official view — of internal amity and unanimity of purpose — was not, and perhaps had never been, entirely realistic.

*　　*　　*

The Festival — Sable said it was the most important of Shadow anniversaries — was held in a large open space not far from the Shadeau: the many miles he had ranged on Wolken, it struck Robert when they arrived there, were now contracted into an ordinary meadow.

The proceedings began with what the children recognized as a historical pageant, for they could by now distinguish variations in Shadow dress, the differences between the sombre purplish robes of the bishops, the faintly luminous garb of the poets and philosophers they had learnt about, and the drab frail-looking armour of the warriors.

One episode — Sable explained — told of a mythical being called Antimetheus, who saved the Shadows from fire by bearing it away into the sky, clutching it to his breast with his bare hands. Another represented in slapstick fashion — Timmy laughed at the performers who carried huge discs before and behind, like sandwich-men — a quarrel between the sun and the moon which ended in the victory of the moon and the eclipse of the sun.

Ballads were sung, and someone read a long narrative poem in blank verse through a megaphone which didn't work very well. The Shadows grew restless, there was some discontented muttering, and the poem came to an abrupt end when one of them grabbed the megaphone out of the speaker's hand and made off with it.

The girls enjoyed what came next: ancient dances, in

which the dancers spun lightly to and fro, circling their partners gracefully, blending together, then passing backwards and forwards through them. The smoothly changing patterns made by their movements, like a kaleidoscope without colour, impressed Jane and Lily as quite beautiful.

'It is the art we are best at,' Sable told them.

*   *   *

Later they walked round the booths and sideshows set up along the edge of the meadow.

'Yum yum!' said Leslie, 'a fair!' said Lily.

Timmy was going to enquire after the Ghost Train but then it struck him that things were ghostly enough as it was. Jane and Lily wanted to have their fortunes told by Madam Vespertine – 'Coming Shadows Cast Their Events Before' said the notice outside her tent – but Robert was firmly opposed to the idea, and Sable didn't seem much in favour.

Nor was she in favour of the switchback, a fearsome structure from which Shadows came tumbling to earth, picking themselves up among tiny shrieks of laughter.

'Too soon for that,' Sable said.

She led them to a booth where you had to throw balls – ping-pong balls, said Timmy – into buckets so that they didn't bounce out again. Some of the Shadows managed to do this, but however gently Leslie and Timmy tossed them, the balls passed right through the flimsy buckets and the man in charge had to scoop them out of the grass beneath.

'Come back next year,' he told them, shaking his head knowingly.

Yes, we're still beyond the pale, Robert punned in private, making a wry face.

But Timmy won a prize at the roulette table, when the wheel stopped at 8, his favourite number this year. Much to his disgust the prize turned out to be a pair of dark glasses.

'Keep them,' Sable advised. 'They'll prove useful one day.'

But he wouldn't be consoled until she had bought them large handfuls of candy-floss, like a highland mist of sugar.

*   *   *

The Shadows had gathered expectantly in rows along two sides of the meadow. Something interesting was going to happen.

Then from one side came a disorderly mob of figures in grey tunics, carrying cardboard representations of flaming brands painted a harmless dull yellow. These figures were shouting and throwing themselves from side to side in a threatening manner.

From the opposite side of the field came an orderly array of Shadow soldiers carrying black shields and tube-like weapons which reminded Robert of the mysterious object in the joke shop. They were dark-throwers, Sable whispered.

Timmy asked where the tanks and armoured cars were, and the rocket-launchers and the bomber planes.

'This war has always been fought hand to hand,' Sable said.

'Person-to-person missiles. . .' muttered Robert.

Sable looked at him closely. 'I think you really understand,' she said, 'don't you?'

To Timmy she said, 'It's really all metaphor. . . this country is given to metaphor.'

'Metaphor,' he said brightly. 'I know what that is — it's signalling with flags.'

Each party advanced on the other — the children had soon understood that the disorderly gang were meant to be humans — amid a good deal of shouting and the soft scuffling of cardboard on tin.

'Dark!' chanted the Shadow soldiers, 'For Darkness and Saint Shadost!' Others cried, 'Chimera!' and 'Ténébreux!'

It wasn't exactly a full-throated roar by human standards, or by those of hungry lions, and certainly not to be compared with the roaring of football fans. But to the children it sounded frighteningly fierce, and the girls clung to Sable. So, in a more reserved way, did Timmy, hoping that none of the spectators would take him for one of the enemy.

The Lightists, the brand-bearing rabble, were eventually put to flight with what appeared to be considerable slaughter, and a brass band marched on to the field. The brass didn't shine or glitter, but the oompah-oompah and the drums sounded unmistakably triumphant.

A famous victory, Robert mused. He wondered which defeat of his race the skirmish represented, which particular disaster or reversal. Or was it wishful thinking on the part of the Shadows? Just a game of toy soldiers? No, he had formed too much respect for them to think it was merely that.

*   *   *

The band had stopped, and there was a pause in the proceedings.

88

Then another procession filed on, by no means so orderly as the Shadow troops, and much quieter than the Lightists. Row after uneven row of ancient Shadows limped slowly on to the field, their heads bowed, many of them with an arm or a leg burned off, supported by their comrades. Their leaders carried black flags drooping towards the ground.

The spectators were silent, some of them wiping away a tear, as these casualties of old battles moved shakily past.

Then they began to sing softly and sadly, a solemn tune which the older children found vaguely familiar.

> *'Lead, kindly Dark, amid the encircling light,*
> *Lead Thou me on. . .'*

Robert was baffled by his emotions. It was like Remembrance Sunday, and the deep, hollow boom of the maroon, and the two-minute silence. Did you feel sorrowful, or angry? Forgiving or vengeful? Or what?

17 · *High Words in the Library*

'What do they *feel*? What sort of exultation? What sort of grief? What do we have in common? And what not? What do we *know*?'

Mr Spock was beginning to be sorry he had made that clever remark about spiritual advances being brought to his notice.

The three were in the Public Library, where for the past couple of hours Mr Spock had busied himself with a large pile of books: the Collected Works of the Oxford English Poets. His task was to produce at short notice a quantitative (prior to a qualitative) breakdown of factors hypothetically relevant to the throwing of light upon the darkness or darkness upon the light in the light or the darkness of those authors most celebrated for their spiritual insights or outlooks. *Id est,* something that just possibly might help.

Fortunately Mr Spock was a very fast reader: upside-down, right way up, or sideways, it was all one to him. Indeed, 'reading' was hardly the right word for what he was doing. His mind was less like a rapier than a computer, but far more valuable to such projects as the present one than the most sophisticated of computers, simply because of its — we mustn't say irrationalities or intuitions, since that would pain him — because of its, well, its large dark bottom. For willy-nilly Mr Spock had inherited from his mixed parentage more than merely one Racial Unconscious. But this was something he preferred not to be too conscious of.

'Study your enemy!' said Inspector Barlow stirringly, as he displayed an extra-large book of X-ray photographs which he had found in the Medical Section. He wanted to do his bit.

'This isn't a jaunt on the Ghost Train!' Herr Brush said in his tartest tones. 'They're not skeletons, you know. We're not just up against a lot of bags of bones!' Time was the enemy, the one nearest at hand, and it seemed to be winning.

Mr Spock was huddled elegantly over his books, his mind ticking away rapidly and almost audibly.

'Listen to this,' he said:

> *'Some there be that shadows kiss;*
> *Such have but a shadow's bliss*

— that's Shakespeare.'

'And listen to this,' retorted Herr Brush:

> *'Some there be that shadows fight;*
> *Such have but a shadow's bite*

— that's Brush!'

'Shush!' said the Librarian, giving them a stern look.

'*Shhushh!*' said the Inspector twice as loudly. He wasn't going to stand by and hear his authority usurped by some date-stamping clerk.

'It's five o'clock,' whispered Herr Brush. 'And we're getting nowhere.' It was an excellent idea, he had no doubt, but it would require years of long winter evenings in the backroom to carry out.

'I'm going as fast as I can,' Mr Spock said, wounded. 'I've got to Swift already. . . There would appear to be rather a large number of Oxford Poets.'

'What's the use of it?' cried Herr Brush in a burst of hysteria. 'Nuances and shades of meaning — misteries and sunnets — umbiguities and noctations — litotes and alliteration — oxies and morons — seelables and blackcents — Light Verse and Dark Ladies —'

'No Talking Allowed in Here!' hissed the Librarian. 'Not to mention shouting.'

'And when you've finished the poets there'll be the Oxford English Novels to work through,' Herr Brush rushed on. He was as close to despair as was in his nature to be, though an ignorant observer would merely have thought him off his head. 'And then the Cambridge Critics —'

He tugged out his pipe. Not that he was thinking of smoking it. More likely, of bashing out his brains with it. It was big enough to do the job.

'Smoking is Not Permitted. And if you continue to make a noise I shall have to ask you to leave.' The Librarian was getting ratty.

'The Law is the Law and it must be respected,' the Inspector uttered in mollifying tones. 'So, not a word more, I promise you.' He pulled out a thermos flask containing tea and offered it to Herr Brush, his finger to his lips. 'This is what you need,' he whispered resoundingly.

'The Consumption of Food and Drink on These Premises is Strictly Forbidden,' snarled the Librarian as he picked up the telephone and started to dial the police.

Mr Spock closed the *Poetical Works Including The*

Plays of Alfred, Lord Tennyson, and they trooped out sheepishly.

'Search is the word,' said Herr Brush, with all the briskness he was able to summon up, 'not re-search.'

18 · A Discovery

It was Sable's wedding day. And she was happy, too happy for a Shadow, perhaps.

The children had been allowed to visit her, while she was preparing herself for the ceremony. To their surprise her gown was white, or something approaching white, the brightest thing they had seen for ages. It almost dazzled them.

Sable explained that it was an old tradition that, if she chose (and generally she didn't), a bride could wear white, despite the revulsion normally felt for the colour. Again, there were various theories to account for this concession: for example, that once upon a time a Shadow prince fell madly in love with a young human girl who had stumbled by chance into the country while fleeing from bandits, and she had steadfastly refused to marry him except in a white robe. From their union, it was said, sprang the greatly loved philanthropist, Witchhazel, who despite her beauty and riches devoted her life to relieving the distresses of the poor and stirring the consciences of the well-to-do.

But Finsterness, said Sable, had his own joking explanation: 'White, because even among us marriage is full of hazards!'

So it was to prove, for him.

*　　　*　　　*

What had added so much to Sable's happiness sprang out of a chance question of Jane's, about the place Sable had come from, and what her brother was like. . .

Sable said that he was the sweetest of brothers, younger than she, but he had looked after her like a father. Their parents had both been killed during some war, she couldn't remember which, when the children were very small. . . Her little brother, for all his cares, was a lively youngster, jolly, always laughing, and full of amusing pranks and far-fetched tales.

'He was such a boy for making up funny stories about the neighbours. . . And for playing with words. . . I remember, he used to go round pretending to be a German so that people would have to address him as Herr Brush. His name was Brush, you see —'

All the children burst out talking at the same time. Herr Brush? Oh *they* knew Herr Brush, they couldn't forget him, there couldn't possibly be two Herr Brushes in the world, not even in all the worlds. . .

'A lovely foxy old pheasant he is,' Timmy assured Sable, shouting to make himself heard. 'I'm almost positive I can remember him buying me an ice-cream, you know. Or even two.'

'But he's an old gentleman,' Jane cried. 'He can't be your little brother! Your little brother would have to be like Leslie here, or Robert.'

'You forget that here we age very slowly, for time passes slowly,' Sable said. Then she made them compose themselves and tell her, one by one, or two by two, in detail, everything they could about her brother Brush.

She wept a little, but still looked happy, as the children rattled on about Herr Brush and Mr Span — Spick — no, Spock, and even about the large Inspector, and then about their parents and Lily's and Leslie's mum, and looking for the twins, and the ice-cream parlour, and the joke shop. All the things they thought they had forgotten till that very moment.

'That's Brush,' she said softly when at last they came to an end. 'That's my darling Brush. He hasn't changed at all. . .'

'His teeth have,' said Timmy gravely as another memory returned to him. 'He can't eat ice-cream because they ache. He ought to go to the dentist before it's too late.'

*   *   *

Sable saw that the children were still far from reconciled to their new life. She knew — she was the only one Finsterness had told — of Robert's determined but vain attempt to escape on Wolken. It had only needed a mention of her lost brother's name and the children's memories had come tumbling back, one after another. The processes of assimilation, the 'natural processes' as the Shadoctrinators termed them, were not working well in their case. And, overjoyed though she was to hear that Brush was alive, her heart was heavy with grief for the children. They had much to suffer before each of them became — as she had become (and she was lucky: she was to marry Finsterness) — a more or less contented Shadow, a being of dimnesses and subdual, of half-emotions, of narrow needs and simple satisfactions. But also, she reminded herself, of repose, of tranquillity and — except for the never-ending war with the Light — of peace.

For her that Shadow life would suffice, even if she weren't happily in love with a Shadow. But for them? They were so young, and she felt so old beside them. They had been stolen away from their rightful lives — 'nasty, brutish and short', one of their great men had said, and so human life was, compared with the life that had become hers. Wilful, selfish, envious and perverse, hurting themselves and others, like meteorites consuming themselves and everything around them, their history was one of brutality and suffering. . . Such terrible energies!

Yet that wasn't the whole story. Even Finsterness, loyal and aboriginal Shadow as he was, didn't believe it was. For after all they did live their lives, they suffered but they enjoyed too. 'A short life and a merry' — that was another saying. An old verse came into her head, though the Shadow in her shrank at its words:

> *'My candle burns at both ends,*
> *It will not last the night.*
> *But ah, my foes, and oh, my friends —*
> *It gives a lovely light.'*

Flesh and blood could stand a lot, it was made to stand a lot. And they were still flesh and blood.

*   *   *

She asked the children if they truly wanted to go back, to return — home.

Yes, they were unanimous. Though Timmy, she noticed, lagged a little behind the others in conviction. That was natural: the younger the child, the weaker the resistance, the less the rootedness. Jane had faltered, but Sable knew why, and knew it didn't really mean very much.

97

She told them that it was considered quite impossible to escape from the country. But, in the very nature of things, only children, newcomers at that, had ever tried, as far as she knew. Otherwise no one ever desired to escape, for where and what would they escape to?

She could help them, but only if they were sure they wanted to try, and only in a small way. She couldn't ask for Finsterness's help — that would be unfair, it might even be disastrous — she couldn't mention it to him. But she knew how to get to what the children called 'the joke shop' — on this side of the frontier it took the form of a modest office, a reception post you might say, which was only used when the guards were alerted to possible 'newcomers' in the neighbourhood. She could guide them there: after that they would have to rely on themselves, and on fortune.

The best time for the escape would be that very evening, while the wedding celebrations were in full swing. The Shadows were not given to intoxication, which they regarded as a peculiarly human form of mental violence, but on such occasions they swallowed down their mild potations readily enough, and their wits were likely to be dulled. Sable warned the children that they must behave normally, betraying no signs of excitement.

'But I was already excited about the wedding,' said Jane, again feeling herself pulled in two directions.

Sable's motives were mixed, as motives so often are. If the children escaped, or even one of them, Robert being the likeliest, then they could take news of her to Brush. She knew it was really her that he was always searching for, still hoping to find, and the children could tell him of her marriage, of her contentment, of her happiness even, and then he would need to worry about her no longer.

But first of all, she told herself, it was for the sake of the children themselves. The older ones were bound fast to earth, as she had been, and she knew what pain that meant. She had spent much time between two worlds, the one dying reluctantly, the other coming to birth so slowly.

'And on the low dark verge of life,' she found herself reciting, 'The twilight of eternal night. . .'

19 · *Marriage and Mayhem*

It was really quite gay, the children decided, quite high-spirited, as spirits went.

In fact for the Shadows a wedding was the equivalent of a carnival in the Caribbean, or *Fasching* in Germany, when for an appointed time riot and disorder are allowed to reign. Every race needs a temporary release from order, routine and propriety. No doubt the rioting and revelling of the Shadows could have graced a Royal Garden Party, or been transported to an English church hall without cause for complaint or raised eyebrows. But everything is relative.

Sable looked entrancing, Jane thought, and Finsterness rather noble in his remote fashion. He had been courteous enough to deny himself dark glasses: most of the guests, for whom the bride's gown posed problems both physical and moral, had protected their eyes in some way. Jane wondered idly whether Hecatus was present − probably not, unless he had finally accepted the fact that Sable was not for him.

Sable prevailed on the master of ceremonies, a worried figure who was plainly unnerved by their presence, to allow the children a small glass each of light greyish wine. They found it cool and pleasant enough, but (as humans would have said) somewhat lacking in body. It was a remarkable indulgence, considering the puritanical attitude of the Shadows towards both drink and children.

The hall was packed with Shadows, conversing gently, bowing to one another, drinking one another's health. At times they are almost civilized, Robert thought to himself. He was hoping that they would get stinking drunk, stagger about, and then fall asleep snoring — he had once seen his father in that state, he suddenly remembered with a gush of affection, when he had come across a bad review of a book of his — but didn't believe there was much chance of it happening. He felt very tense, and was nervous lest the Shadows might notice it, especially Finsterness who had eyes in the back of his head and probably elsewhere.

'I feel scared,' Leslie had whispered. 'If they catch us, they're bound to punish us. . .'

'We shan't get caught,' he had replied, with a show of confidence.

*　　*　　*

After the drinking and chatting came the throwing of confetti — it was black, the children observed, and looked fine as it hung on Sable's gown. The pronouncement of the marriage vows, Sable told them, would come right at the end.

Scraps of long-forgotten poetry kept drifting into Sable's head: she guessed it had something to do with Brush, who had the habit of quoting lines of deathless verse, as he put it, to ward off verseless death.

She whispered teasingly into Finsterness's ear, 'The prince of darkness is a gentleman' — which appeared to please him for he thereupon kissed her gently, taking care not to disturb the chaplet she wore, made of dark green

101

leaves interwoven with small dark-red flowers, purple buds and the white blossom of the blackthorn.

Aloud she spoke:

> *'I will encounter darkness as a bride,*
> *And hug it in mine arms.'*

A hum of admiring approbation arose from the gathered guests, who little knew where the words came from. Finsterness knew, for he had always maintained that if your enemy was worth fighting, he was worth studying too. But he only smiled — it was after all a nicely turned compliment — saying, 'Yes, it must be admitted that they do have some rather good poets.'

They gathered to mix with their guests, and Sable took the opportunity to tell Robert to make sure the five children stayed close together, and to watch out for her signal: she would wave her white wedding handkerchief up and down. It wouldn't be long now.

*   *   *

Solemn expressions had come over the faces of the company, and all were silent, except for the ancient gentleman who was doing his tremulous best to cope with the simplicities of the solemnization of matrimony.

There was no mention — though the children, being inexperienced in such matters, were not aware of the omission — of matrimony as ordained for the procreation of children. Nor of it being a remedy against sin, something which in their personal lives the Shadows were barely conscious of. But there was a lot about mutual society, help and comfort: that was what they prized and looked for.

'Therefore if any man can. . . show any just cause. . .

why they may. . . not lawfully be joined together. . .'
The old Shadow's quavering voice died away, then started up again painfully. Really, Jane told herself, they should have picked somebody who sounded more cheerful. 'Let him now speak. . . or else hereafter. . . for ever hold his peace.'

During the ensuing pause, prescribed though it may have been, the old Shadow appeared to have fallen asleep. Jane wondered whether he thought he had to wait for ever.

Suddenly a figure broke through the surrounding circle, with a violence of movement that alarmed even the children. Several of the guests, lost in the dreamy solemnity, were knocked to the floor.

'Hecatus!' they heard Sable cry out in a terrified voice.

The Shadow drew from his cloak a small cylindrical object which struck Robert as familiar yet not immediately identifiable. 'Cigars already?' he wondered, recalling the wedding of his mother's younger brother. Hardly. . . Then it came to him — yes, that was what it was — the last thing to be expected here — a thin battery-torch, the kind carried in the top pocket like a pen. . .

Hecatus pointed the torch at Finsterness. No one did anything, no one moved. Perhaps they were paralysed by the shock of such sudden and unlooked-for violence; perhaps they failed to recognize what he held in his hand.

Robert unfroze. Some old instinct, missing in the Shadows assembled there, came quick and alive in him. He catapulted forward, yelling 'That's light!' — as much horror and urgency in his voice as if it were a live bomb instead of a small battery-torch from Woolworth's. 'Look out, it will kill!'

103

Hecatus had his finger on the button when Robert cannoned into him. The torch fell, and Robert felt himself sinking partially into Hecatus, one of his arms going right through the floor.

Finsterness was protecting Sable, Sable was protecting Finsterness. Then the Shadows took in the meaning of Robert's shriek and came to help him. Plain-clothes guards who had been placed discreetly among the guests, probably to keep an eye on the children, threw themselves on Hecatus. He fought like a demon, flinging himself this way and that, his figure turning an almost radiant black, but he was overpowered and dragged away.

'The Black Hole for him!' Timmy remarked grimly and loudly. If this was part of the wedding ceremony, then it was the best part so far, he reckoned.

The Shadows were appalled — less by what might have happened than by what had undeniably happened. That a respected and highly placed Shadow like Hecatus could behave in such a way: that he could deliberately choose such a weapon, the weapon of the enemy, indeed — on however small a scale — the enemy itself incarnate: and thus imperil all their lives for the sake of some little private aim! Mutual help and comfort? It was unheard of — even the wildest of legends told of nothing to compare with this! It was — there was only one word for it — nothing short of *human*!

Robert took advantage of their shock and confusion to pocket the torch. Just in case — though he hoped he wouldn't have to use it on anyone.

The ancient Shadow, so rudely interrupted at the climax of his duties, had collapsed. Heart attack probably, the poor old fellow, thought Robert: they said that even the word 'Light' could finish off the extremely elderly. But we all have to go sooner or later, he told himself, as Finsterness and others clustered round the prostrate figure.

At that moment he caught sight of Sable, waving her handkerchief as if to give herself air, and then moving nimbly towards the door. Robert joined the other four, and they raced quietly after her.

20 · *Escape!*

Sable led them quickly out of the Shadeau, through the thin wood which surrounded it, down a hill, alongside a dark and slow-moving river. They saw a few farm-workers in the distance, but these went about their business, paying no attention to the fugitives.

Brambles and reeds whipped at their ankles, but offered no resistance. Once a sudden sound startled them, close at hand. But it was only the cry of a night-bird, sad and full of obscure longing.

Robert thought about the deadly weapon he was carrying. If they were stopped, perhaps it would be enough to point the torch threateningly and explain quickly what it was. He hoped the threat would be sufficient, but he believed that if necessary he could bring himself to press the button that operated the torch. Let it not be Finsterness, though, he added.

*   *   *

A strange lethargy was settling upon the children. Eager though their minds were to hasten on and away, their limbs were reluctant to carry them. Leslie tripped over his own feet, or his feet tripped over each other, and lost a shoe. It wouldn't have hurt him to go bare-foot, but he argued that having only one shoe was like being a single twin, and only the very poorest people went around in their bare feet. The shoe was found, and Lily struggled to get it back on.

Timmy collapsed on the grass, with a loud groan, and had to be hauled up by his brother. Among other fears and anxieties, Robert was thinking of how people who fell asleep in the snow never woke up again.

A scrap of some old verse or song floated indistinctly into Sable's head — Brush, she thought, Brush can't be very far away — something to do with Babylon, how did it go?

> *'How many miles to Babylon?*
> *Threescore miles and ten,'*

Jane told her. A long, long way away. She threw herself into Sable's arms, whispering that she didn't want to go any further, it was too far, couldn't she stay with Sable?

Sable shook her gently. 'But you must go on, you know,' she said, 'just a little further,' and then, as the words came back to her,

> *'If your heels are nimble and light,*
> *You will get there by candlelight.'*

The rhyme worked like magic. The children were moving again, running with Sable.

*   *   *

The border post was a bare, sinister place, but at least it seemed to be deserted. Merely a few uncomfortable chairs, a table with tin mugs, some dark-throwers stacked in a corner.

'Now I must go back,' said Sable, as firmly as she could. 'My life is here. . . There's nothing more I can do for you. But I'm sure there will be someone on the other side who can help you. Perhaps even my Brush. If so, kiss him for me.'

She kissed the children in turn. To Robert she said, 'Thank you for saving Finsterness.' Then, 'May the Light always be good to you, children.'

And then she had gone.

*   *   *

It was so very dark. But they went into the darkness, and found themselves passing through a long corridor. Robert chased round them like a sheep-dog, and then the corridor opened out and they realized they were at the rear of the front window of the joke shop.

They could detect the door by which they had first entered from the street: they wrestled with the handle, but the door was locked fast, and there was no key.

They scrambled on to the dusty counter, trying not to step on the spider or the other barely recognizable articles that lay there.

As far as they could tell, there was no one about on the other side. Even if there had been, Robert thought unhappily, would they have noticed five lacklustre little faces behind the grimy glass? The children were still in Shadow territory.

Leslie and Timmy were hammering their fists against the window, but they might as well have been pummelling solid rock-face, or – for their efforts made not the slightest noise – a thick wall of rubber.

'If they catch us now,' moaned Lily, 'it will be the Black Hole for ever,' groaned Leslie.

Jane was silent. She was missing Sable, she had felt safe with Sable. Wouldn't it have been better to stay at the wedding party, with Sable, with Finsterness? It was cold and dirty in the joke shop, and frightening. It was the loneliest place of all.

Robert too could feel menace in the air, and he sensed himself weakening before it. This was the thin dividing line between one world and another, the scene of much violence and terror in the past, and ghosts lingered there.

'I've got an idea!' he cried. 'The torch — if I shine it through the window perhaps somebody will see it and come to see what's going on.'

The children cheered up, they thought it an excellent idea. Robert himself wasn't so certain. They too were vulnerable to light now — how vulnerable there was no way of knowing — and if the light should reflect back from the glass and strike one of them. . .

There was only one way of finding out. He told them to stand well away, in the corners of the dark display counter, and keep their eyes closed tight.

I bet Finsterness would be proud of me, he thought — and somehow the thought gave him courage. He pointed the torch and pressed the button.

21 · 'I have a feeling'

'Not so fast!' cried Inspector Barlow pathetically.

'In fact we are moving rather slowly,' Mr Spock pointed out.

'I still think there's something peculiar about that dingy old shop. Something wrong,' murmured Herr Brush, dragging himself along painfully.

'That boring shop of yours! We've passed it three times in the last three hours,' said Inspector Barlow. 'And not a sign of anything out of the ordinary — let alone illegal. Just a silly old shop closed for the night.' He sighed heavily. 'I had better remind you that a police officer's duty — and a police officer is what, to outward appearances, I am supposed to be — is to see that that which is unlocked is locked — and not the other way about.'

They stopped to lean against a wall. They were dirty and tired and dejected. Even Mr Spock's feet were hurting.

'I have a feeling about that place,' Herr Brush insisted doggedly. 'An intuition. What you might call an into-ition.'

'Feelings, intuitions!' Mr Spock cast his eyes up to-wards heaven. 'I shall never succeed in understanding you. . . All the same' — he didn't want to hurt Herr Brush's fine feelings — 'we might as well have another look at it.'

'Yes,' Mr Spock went on more enthusiastically. 'Joke shop. . . It is conceivable that they have — what do you call that curious phenomenon? — a sense of humour. Something in common with you Earthlings? It wouldn't be the only thing. . .'

The Inspector grumbled half-heartedly. Then they turned about and hurried back the way they had come.

22 · A Sneeze in Time

'The battery,' Lily gasped, 'won't last much longer,' sighed Leslie. They could have been talking of themselves.

'I'm doing my best to save it.' Robert had been switching the torch on briefly, then off again for a longer period. It appeared to be dark on the other side, but that could have been the filthy glass, or some strange extension of Shadow-space, or simply their own condition. For all he knew it might be blazing noon out there, and then nobody would notice the slender ray of light.

Jane was holding Timmy, who had fallen asleep, or half-asleep, in her arms. It seemed to be growing steadily colder. And darker. She could only make out Robert's shape when he switched the torch on. Her strength, she knew, was ebbing away.

On – off, on – off, on – off, went the torch.

*　　*　　*

'Look!' exclaimed Herr Brush as they turned the corner. 'A tiny light, flashing on and off – there's someone inside!'

'Now that,' said Mr Spock, 'is what I would call a logical deduction.'

They ran to the window.

'Can't see anyone,' Inspector Barlow said.

'But then, we wouldn't *see* anyone, would we? You know the effects. . . ' He was extremely excited. 'I'm sure they're there. I can feel it in my bones. My hairs are standing on end.' They were: it was a gift of his.

'I believe you're right. I can make out something or somebody. Miles away, one would think,' said Mr Spock, showing signs if not of excitement then of marked interest. His eyes were abnormally sharp, though not as keen as his hearing.

They tried the door, but it wouldn't budge.

'I had better send for a locksmith,' the Inspector said. 'We enjoy the services of a reformed housebreaker. . . Or did he say he was going to Loch Lomond for his holidays?'

'There's no time to send for anything!' cried Brush. 'Every second counts — if it is the children in there, by now they'll be on their last legs. Can we smash the window?'

'In the circumstances you have my express authority to effect an entry by those means,' the Inspector assured him graciously. 'I shall take full responsibility. . . Oh, I see what you mean. Here, let me try — I'm the biggest and strongest.'

He took several paces backwards, threw his overcoat round his head and shoulders, and then hurled himself sideways at the window. There was a dull thud, and the Inspector flew head over heels into the gutter.

'Heroic,' groaned Mr Spock. 'The Charge of the Heavy Brigade!'

'There's more here than meets the eye,' remarked the Inspector, dusting himself down and counting his limbs.

'Of course there is!' Brush squeaked in anguish.

'Do you have a pain?' Mr Spock enquired of him

113

gravely. Imperturbable himself, he frequently under-estimated the perturbability of his colleagues.

'Yes,' moaned Brush, 'in the window.'

Then Brush had an idea. 'A high-pitched sound will sometimes shatter glass, you know. Don't you carry a whistle with you, Inspector?'

'Invariably,' said the Inspector. 'I wouldn't be without one.' He took his whistle off its chain and handed it to Brush. 'Your wind is better than ours. Do your best, old fellow. That whistle is Supertonic. Highly recommended.'

Brush blew and blew. But nothing happened, except that the Inspector got a terrible pain in his head and begged him to desist.

*   *   *

The children could just see their would-be rescuers through the screen of dirt. Instinctively they moved out of the way when the large form of Inspector Barlow came hurtling towards them. The next moment he bounced off the glass as if it were really rubber, and disappeared from sight.

'Robert!' whispered Jane urgently. 'I think they're coming – the Shadows.'

He listened, and there was a distant echoing, the clip-clop of hooves, only audible because the horsemen had already entered the dark corridor which led to the back of the shop.

Timmy was awake. He had struggled up and was jumping about to egg on the Inspector. He squashed the poor spider flat, then found himself skidding as if on skates – he had stepped on the mechanical mouse.

There came a crash as something broke into pieces. Then a cloud of dust rose about the children, and they

114

started to sneeze. It was a Family Size jar of Genuine Old Sneezing Powder that Timmy had sent flying.

Robert sneezed so hard that he dropped the torch, and it rolled away into the darkness. Jane sneezed, searching for her handkerchief which she had been taught to use on such occasions. Lily began a family-size sneeze, and Leslie concluded it a second later. Timmy was sneezing in his usual generous fashion, and almost enjoying it.

It was true that the children's sneezes were rather faint, mere shadows of sneezes, but they went on sneezing, and shaking and bumping into one another, until at last their sneezes synchronised. And then there erupted one great joint sneeze.

The Shadows, who had slackened when they heard the strange and violent noises, were upon them and reining in their horses, when there came a second crash, much louder, like the crack of a gigantic whip.

The shop window had shattered, and bits of it fell out into the street. Arms came through, groping for the children.

'Come on, my darlings,' shouted Brush. 'No time to lose! Mind the nasty edges if you can, but hurry up!'

Robert pushed the others through the largest gap in the window. 'Never mind your hankie,' he said to Jane, 'just get going!'

'Are you really real?' Timmy asked as Mr Spock lifted him down into the street.

He sneezed once more, almost blowing Mr Spock over.

'Out of the mouth of babes and sucklings!' said Mr Spock admiringly.

115

'Out of their noses!' chortled Herr Brush, rubbing his own in satisfaction. He had one arm round Lily's waist and the other round Leslie's. He seemed to be looking for other arms to put round other waists.

23 · *A Red Face at Night*

Actually it was early evening and the sun was low in the sky, yet the children found themselves squinting painfully. Such bright colours everywhere — colours they had never dreamt of, or had dreamt of a long, long time ago!

But they were young, and it didn't take much time for them to adjust to the harsh new brilliance.

'What an awfully red face you have!' said Timmy to the Inspector.

'All the better to rouse you out of your dreams with, you young ruffian,' the Inspector replied with uncommon joviality. 'A red face at night is the lost child's delight.'

Only a moment earlier, the children had been at the end of their tether: utterly exhausted, drained of their strength and will by the negative force-field that hung over the joke shop, too enfeebled to step through a shattered window and out of one world into another.

But now, her words falling over one another in her excitement, Jane was telling Herr Brush about Sable, and Finsterness, and happiness, and never forgetting her brother — and Jane didn't forget the kiss she had promised to pass on to him.

'From Sable,' she whispered, and blushed slightly.

Huge tears rolled down Brush's cheeks and into

his big smile, and Jane began to fear he might drown in them.

'A good man, this Finsterness?' he said at last. 'A good Shadow, I should say. . . Well, happiness isn't easily come by wherever you are. . .' Then he added enigmatically, 'Learn distinct to know, O Mortals, the difference between States and Individuals of those States. . . How hard that is to learn distinct. . .'

Timmy was gabbling on about Robert and how he had been so brave and smart and fought with the bad Shadow Hecatus while all the other Shadows just stood around and did nothing except gnash their gums and look silly.

Lily and Leslie were complaining to the Inspector about the hours and hours of rotten lessons they had suffered, and how it oughtn't to be allowed. Then Lily remembered she had left her dolls behind, and Leslie remembered an elaborate sandcastle he had left unfinished, and they both turned sulky and difficult.

The Inspector showed little interest in their grievances. 'No doubt your mother the widow-woman Lacey will be highly gratified to have you back,' he remarked. 'Though heaven knows why.'

'I want,' cried Lily, remembering what it was they wanted, 'my mum,' cried Leslie indignantly.

Robert hadn't spoken a word. He was too old to cry, even if he had known what to cry about. At the moment he didn't altogether know what to think or feel. He wasn't even sure where he was.

'Trees and grass,' he muttered. Then he said, in sudden surprise, 'But you haven't changed — you haven't changed at all!'

'We try our best to improve,' Mr Spock remarked

apologetically. 'It isn't easy at our time of life.'

'I mean, you ought to look older than when we saw you last. That was ages ago.'

'That, to be precise,' said the Inspector pompously, taking out a large pocket-watch, 'was more or less exactly twenty-four hours ago, give or take a couple of hours or so. . . And we have been searching for you without respite ever since you made off in that surreptitious and highly irregular manner. . .'

'God bless you all,' put in Brush, his heart full.

'You have acquitted yourselves most creditably,' Mr Spock informed the children in general. Turning to Robert, he added, '*You* have changed, a little. . . And when you are older, perhaps you will recall something of what has passed — and think of us, for we can do with the help of brave men —'

'Enough!' Brush interrupted. 'Leave the future to look after itself — you're not an employment bureau, my dear Spock! What they have to do now is forget. . .'

'A man's life of any worth,' Mr Spock remarked judiciously, 'is a continual allegory. . . I quote an Oxford English Poet.'

'Allegories, allergies!' exclaimed Brush impatiently. 'You are far too metaphysical, Spock! Let's just be physical for a while, shall we?'

Robert said, 'I shan't forget. Not everything. I don't *think* I shall.'

The others were beginning to forget already.

'We want to go home,' wailed Lily and Leslie in unison, like children who have stayed up far too late at night.

'I'll see to you two,' said the Inspector. 'It's on my way home, and the widow-woman Lacey brews a famous cup of tea. . .' He said something to his friends about procuring an emergency demolition order for the joke shop first thing in the morning. 'Bring up a bulldozer. . . Bang, wallop, crash, tinkle. . . Then the joke will be on them.'

He caught hold of the twins. 'Come along, you young rapscallions. . . Heading straight for Reform School, that's what you are, and Redbrick Varsity and Television Documentaries, I shouldn't be at all surprised!'

'See you,' said Lily languidly, 'sometime,' said Leslie with a yawn, and they waved wearily to the other children as the Inspector bore them off.

'Breaking and Exiting at your age!' he was grumbling, 'Grievous Shadowy Harm! Unlawful Possession of Sneezing Powder!' He had the twins by the ear, but he couldn't have been hurting them, Brush said, since he was wearing his special padded police gloves for handling strayed china and runaway babies. And in any case the feeling hadn't altogether come back into their ears as yet.

The Inspector, Brush assured them, was really very pleased with the way the affair had turned out – for one thing, it would mean promotion for him.

'A good day's work,' said Brush, wiping away a last lingering tear.

24·'*Who'd believe them?*'

It had seemed like years. It still did. Well, like months at least. But in this new world, with its loudly ticking clocks, its booming church bells and its noisy bustling buses, even twenty-four hours was quite bad enough!

What would their father say?

What would they say to their father?

Though he had come closest of them all to sinking into that other existence, Timmy was the quickest to return from it. He clapped his hands together with immense satisfaction. He was happy to hear his shoes banging against the pavement as they ran towards the common.

Once there he grabbed at tall grasses and twigs, feeling an unaccountable pleasure in getting his fingers firmly round them. Until a thorn ran into his hand, and they had to stop while Jane squeezed it out.

They looked back, and there were Brush and Mr Spock, watching them. They waved, and the men waved back.

'Nobody will ever believe us,' panted Robert as they ran on. 'Nobody.'

'But there's Brush and Mr Spock and the Inspector — they'll tell Daddy that — well, that we haven't been really naughty. . .'

'I'm not sure they'll tell him anything,' said Robert gravely. 'Who'd believe *them*? They are a bit out of the ordinary. And what if we can't find them again?' He suspected that they were busy men.

Timmy was moaning about the thorn – he wasn't used to things hurting in that way, and it seemed most unfair.

'P'raps Foxy Brush and the others are only pigments of our image-nation. . .' he managed to bring out drowsily. It was years past his bedtime.

Robert and Jane agreed that they might well be figments of somebody's imagination, though only Jane was halfway to believing it.

'I hope there's something nice for supper.' Timmy perked up as this new thought occurred to him.

'You'll be lucky!' Robert said grimly.

'We could have stayed where we were and been heroes,' Timmy said, as a last brief flash of darkness sped through him. 'With medals and a pension.'

'There are times when I think your brains have gone to your head.' Robert gave a passable imitation of the Inspector addressing Mr Spock more in sorrow than anger. 'But why don't *you* explain everything to Daddy? Then you'll be a real hero!'

25 · The Absolute End

They stepped cautiously through the little front garden and were just inside the hall when their father appeared at the top of the stairs and switched on the light. He was in his dressing-gown, uncombed and unshaven, and he looked dreadfully agitated.

'You see, Daddy. . .' Robert began, with no idea of how he was going to end.

'That's *it*!' their father cried. 'All over! Finished! The absolute and final end!'

'We hope you weren't too worried, Daddy,' Jane started in her sweetest voice, 'but. . .'

'Worried? Ha! Of course I was worried. What do you imagine? I was worried out of my mind!' He waved his arms about tragically. 'I couldn't see how it would ever come out right. . . But then I did. And it did. . .' He smirked modestly, then put on a highly serious expression. 'So the book's done at long last. It's *there*!' He beamed broadly down on them.

'Oh, that *is* good news!' Jane exclaimed, dutifulness assisted by relief. 'Can we be the very first to read it, Daddy? And when is Sa — when's Mummy coming back?'

'Oh yes, you can read it if you like,' their father replied in the far-away and rather bored voice of the great artist weary after his labours. 'And your mother's coming back today. Or is it tomorrow? On the midnight train.'

With somewhat more enthusiasm he added, 'Believe it or not, I haven't had a bite of solid food for twenty-four hours — I'm feeling famished — a shadow of my former self.' He rubbed his hands together. 'Let's see what we can dig up in the kitchen.'

'Very odd,' Timmy mumbled to himself, not knowing whether he was hungrier or tireder. 'Or is it really, when you come to think about it?'